# KARMIC ASTROLOGY

# KARMIC ASTROLOGY

## THE KARMA OF THE NOW

Volume IV
In A Series By

# MARTIN SCHULMAN

SAMUEL WEISER, INC.
York Beach, Maine

First published in 1979 by
Samuel Weiser, Inc.
Box 612
York Beach, Maine 03910

Fifth printing, 1985

ISBN 0-87728-416-4
Library of Congress Catalog Card Number: 83-104490

Printed in the United States by
Mitchell-Shear, Inc.

*. . . To you whose unquenchable thirst for knowledge and enlightenment
serves as a ceaseless fountain of inspiration to us all.*


*. . . To you, who can read the laws of nature between the lines of life.*


*. . . To my dearest little Princess, Penny Sue
who is "The Now."*

## Author's Note

The "Now" is an extremely delicate state of consciousness; difficult to achieve and easy to lose. It is the pure essence of what astrology tries to reach. Therefore, instead of describing certain astrological factors in terms of how they manifest, this text depicts the ways in which an individual can become one with the natural harmony of planetary energies.

Although any book is symbolic communications through language, in this book the reader is asked to see beyond the words into the subtle vibration that is forever creating the "Now" experience.

Martin Schulman

# TABLE OF CONTENTS

# INTRODUCTION

In Volumes, I, II, and III of this series, much attention was given to specific parts of the horoscope (i.e., the nodes, retrogrades, and the part of Fortune). In this book, the framework of reference is different. It centers around the individual, and the ways in which he can use his planetary energies to his best advantage.

There is no question that an individual experiences Karma from other lifetimes. He experiences Karma from his past actions in this life as well and he is also a creator of Karma every moment. It is in this role that it becomes very important for a person to learn the meaning of the moment, for it is from such a concept of life that "The Now" is born.

An individual can spend his entire life searching for what he was in a former incarnation. He may be fortunate enough to find out, or he may delude himself into thinking certain thoughts and then subconsciously creating the circumstances which prove those thoughts to be true to himself. In either case, he is not getting in touch with the real meaning of life unless he realizes that his ability to locate himself in the here and now every moment is where his greatest functioning capacity develops. And through this development of his functioning capacity, his evolution unfolds.

It is extremely easy to blame one's failures on past life Karma, or to put one's inability to cope with every day life situations to chart inadequacies. But this never was, nor must it be allowed to become, either a byproduct of Astrological reasoning or one of the effects of Astrology as a predictive science. If it does, Astrology is doomed to failure; for its gift to humanity is to help man help himself, rather than give him excuses for why he cannot.

Karma exists. It is very real. But it is not beyond man's ability to deal with and overcome. It is important to realize that the past and the future have less to do with man's ability to function and his enjoyment of life than what he does with the "Now." Naturally, the past and future have a strong influence over how an individual perceives the "Now" but—and here is the fascinating point—they don't have to! There is no question that it is extremely difficult to ignore yesterday and not think about tomorrow. And, in a further refinement of this, to ignore a minute ago and not worry about a minute from now. However, with work and discipline, it is possible for a person to do this.

When he does, it does not mean that the past and future do not exist. They do. That is a reality. But he neither lingers in what he has already done or failed to do, nor worries about what he has to do. He simply does, acts, and becomes! He has no time to analyze his actions because that means going back to his past again. He has no time to feel insecure, because that means worrying about his future. Instead he has all the time in the world to live his present reality.

He will be living out his Karma, but he will not be spending years bemoaning his fate, or trying to live the Karma of others rather than his own. He can accept failures and successes, for they are fleeting things which always change. Interestingly enough, when he starts living this way, a good deal of what he thought was Karma starts dropping off because it was, in fact, nothing more than the thoughts he absorbed from others which he thought were his own. Increasingly, he begins to realize what his Karma actually is, because he is not seeking to find out. Nor is he seeking to mix his Karma so much with others that he can never know it.

This form of living makes an individual unbelievably productive and creative. The extent of his output is beyond imagination. For what actually happens is that all the useless and dissipating areas where he would normally put his energies no longer drain him, nor sway him from the reality of his present moment! He grows more vivid, more centered, and more aware not only of his own beauty within, but of all the beauty in the world around him.

# Chapter One

# WHAT IS KARMA REALLY ABOUT?

Whenever an idea becomes widespread in world consciousness its original meaning changes. In fact, the more an idea gains acceptance, the more distant it can become from its original meaning, context, and source. Such has been the case with Karma which is not even an idea, a concept or a thought but rather a Cosmic Law. As more and more people in the world accept the fact that this law exists, there is a greater tendency for the law itself to get twisted as each person interprets it through his own level of understanding.

If a thousand people were asked what Karma is, the tremendous array of answers would be amazing to hear. Even more amazing would be the complexities attached to the very simple essence of this Universal Law.

In order to clearly understand what Karma is, we can trace its meaning from three basic sources and then synthesize these into the most meaningful blend of what actually is the essence at the very core of the Law of Karma.

First, we have the words of Gautama Buddha several thousand years ago when he said, "You are what you think having become what you thought." What did he mean by this profound statement?

Man is always questioning what he is. The fact is that from moment to moment, what he is, changes. And it is these numerous changes that make him wonder if there is anything constant to him at all. If a man "is what he thinks," then as his thoughts change from moment to moment and day to day, so does he! If a man thinks "I am hungry" then that is what he is at the time he thinks it. The moment he no longer thinks it, he is no longer a product of that thought. If a man thinks "I am tired," "I am evil," "I am poor," then he is all of these things. This occurs because there is a very strong tendency for him to believe that what he thinks is the truth. Thus, having belief in one's thoughts about one's self, an individual then identifies with his beliefs and actually becomes all he thinks. If the same pattern of thought is perpetuated for many years, it becomes even more believable to the person who thinks it. Thus, extended thought patterns along any one particular path will lead a person to believe not only that he is on that path, but that it is the only path he can see.

Let us use the analogy of hunger once again, because there are so many forms of hunger that literally everyone has experienced it in one way or another. Consider two individuals about to eat a piece of cake. The first person stares at the cake and instantly has thoughts of conflict. "I want the cake but I know it is going to make me fat." When this person eats the cake, his body will assimilate the food with the same nervousness that was provoked by his thinking. Thus, an unconscious tendency not to want to admit to one's self that one has eaten the cake along with psychological disappointments in one's self for having eaten it, both stemming from the original thought that the cake is harmful, create a situation in which the contact between the cake and the body makes the cake the ruler and the body the servant.

Meanwhile, the second individual contemplating eating the cake looks at it as a source of joy. It is God's food provided for man to fill his needs for sustenance, beauty and vitality. Every crumb in that cake will harmonize with every cell in his body in the most beautiful proportions because the body and the cake are in harmony. This second type of individual never seems to become overweight regardless of what he eats. The first individual can gain several pounds from a single ice cream cone. Here we see a perfect example of what Buddha meant by the words "You are what you think, having become what you thought."

Thus, the first principle of Karmic Law is based on thought. How simple it would be to change one's life merely by changing one's thoughts. But the truth is that no thought is an island unto itself. Always one thought leads to another which leads to another which leads to another which ultimately leads the individual in the direction of his thoughts. Thus, as the years go by it is inevitable that one actually does become "all he has thought."

It is interesting to note that the longer one ascribes to a particular line of thought, the more he brings into his life the kinds of individuals whose own thoughts multiply his original idea. Thus, he is never alone in his thinking. Instead, through the tendency to share his thoughts with others, there is always a growing body of thought in mass consciousness which supports the individual's idea of who he is. He will vibrate to those who believe as he does and shy away from those whose beliefs are different. Every time his thoughts about who he is are threatened, he will draw further back into his past seeking out the very individuals whose present thoughts will reinforce all he used to be. This is one of man's greatest weaknesses—his tendency to avoid overcoming habitual thought patterns.

Even when man is on the path of spiritual growth, he doubts himself every time he sees thoughts in others which are similar to thoughts he used to have himself. This happens because when he believed in those thoughts strongly, he felt it his obligation, his duty and his way of fulfilling his sense of feeling needed, to pass them along to others. Testing the correctness of his own ideas, he tried to convince others that his thoughts were valid.

Now comes the interesting part. Since so much of Karma is based on the effects of what one has thought in the past, then in order to overcome outmoded thought patterns an individual must consider the effects he has caused in other people's lives by trying to impress his own past thoughts upon them. In small measure he has become a part of them, for as they sift and sort out their own individual problems they will draw on many sources for their answers. And one of these sources will be the words he has spoken to them in the past. Because of this, it is cosmically, mathematically, and physically impossible for any individual to rise completely above his own Karma until every other individual whose life he has touched has risen above their Karma in the way he has touched them!

This brings us to the second interpretation of Karma which comes from Newton's Law of Physics, "For every action there must be an equal and opposite reaction." Man is sometimes an actor, a doer, a creator of his life while at other times he is receptive and susceptible to the effects of all he has created. Thus, sometimes he is an actor while at other times he is a reactor. Still, he is very much part of the Law of Cause and Effect.

One of the most interesting ways of understanding this comes from a very common misconception about "talent." Those who are not talented often look upon those who *are* as possessing a kind of mystical air of genius about them; a very special type of aura, a gift. But the talented artist displaying his paintings, his sculpture, his music or his poetry knows that talent is not any of these things at all. He plays a song well because through thousands of hours and perhaps hundreds of months he has trained himself to become master over his instrument.

It is at this point that one might argue that even though it takes thousands of hours to develop a talent some individuals tend to display a greater ease in certain areas than others right from the beginning. There are music students who in their very first lesson show a higher awareness of what music is about than what is normally expected of them. There are art students, who in their very first painting, far surpass beginnner expectations. There are Astrology students who in their very first course are asking questions which show advanced knowledge, often beyond that of their teacher, while other students will have to retake the beginning course again in order to develop a basic understanding of the subject. These facts, rather than negating the law of Cause and Effect, point even stronger to the concept of reincarnation. Within a few short weeks, it becomes very easy for an Astrologer to know which of his or her students has studied Astrology in a prior life; as well as which students are experiencing it for the first time. However, even these students, with proper application and years of serious study, can one day acquire what will appear to others to be tremendous astrological talent. Their eventual mastery over the subject will not come as some strange mystical gift but rather as the direct effect of all of their causal efforts.

Everywhere, this law of Cause and Effect is working, but what seems to be less obvious is that the exact scientific principle, "For every action there must be an equal and opposite reaction," applies constantly to human life. In our everyday relationships, it is easy to see reactions to our actions. But it is much more difficult to understand that the sum total of the reactions we experience are exactly equal to the actions we put out. In other words, imput and output in the long run must always balance out. The reason this seems to be so disguised is because it is entirely possible for individual A to give much more love to individual B than B is capable of returning to A. In such an instance the law of Cause and Effect seems personally doubtful to individual A who appears to be giving more. Still further, the proportionate reaction to every action seems even further out of the question. But, because the universe operates according to very specific cosmic laws, individual A will sooner or later receive more love from individuals C, D, or E, than he himself is capable of giving. When the sum total of debits and credits of human relationships are added up, the bottom line of each column is always a balance of equality.

Sensing this type of boomerang effect, society throughout the world, likes to teach its children the Golden Rule, "Do unto others as you would have them do unto you." In a simpler way, this is just another version of the same scientific principle that for every action one can expect an equal and opposite reaction. If an individual tries to raise his consciousness, through meditation, contemplation, or any other form of esoteric study, he will automatically become confronted with all of the forces in the world which try to lower his consciousness. Thus, as a person begins to vibrate in the direction of more positive energies he automatically becomes more sensitive and must confront the negative energies that represent an equal and opposite reaction to his actions.

In Lao Tsu's famous work *Tao Tse Ching,* the question is asked, "What is a good man?" And, it is answered, "The teacher of a bad man." It goes on to ask, "What is a bad man?" "A good man's charge." If man tries purposefully to be "good," he is always confronted with men who are trying to be "bad." If man is avoiding the goodness in himself, he is unconsciously inviting into his life, all those who will teach him "goodness." The reason why this law of Action and Reaction, Cause and Effect, is so difficult to see is mostly because of the time factor. One normally expects reaction to follow action within a reasonable amount of time so that an observable, logical connection can be made between the two. When the time factor between action and reaction is extended over days, months, or years, many individuals try to explain away the law of Cause and Effect by the word "coincidence." This word "coincidence" is man's obstacle to overcome if he is to understand universal truth. From whatever place an individual draws his understanding, whether his roots be mathematical, scientific, philosophical, religiously oriented, or founded in some varied mixture of all of these, the fact is that "coincidence" is impossible. When one looks at his life from a very personal point of view, it becomes easy to assume that coincidence exists everywhere; for his bundle of unfulfilled desires agitates him so that he has little perspective in understanding anything that does not directly relate to the fulfillment of his desires. But, when man can step out of himself and see the world as it truly is, he begins to notice that, in fact, there are many worlds—and each individual is living within the laws of Cause and Effect, Action and Reaction, from the perspective that he can perceive through his own lifespace. Thus, people talk at each other, but rarely to each other. Still, this is action, and it causes reaction. The lack of understanding that results from it causes each individual to seek others to explain the ideas that they were not able to transmit or receive to those individuals vibrating in worlds inharmonious with their own.

Man never fully understands the extent of his power, for he perceives his own self-created world more often than he does the totality of worlds that make up the universe. If a man in America buys a pair of imported shoes, he is indirectly helping to feed a family in a foreign country who he may never meet. Nevertheless, he has helped to raise the economy of the foreign country and at the same time enabled the family that directly benefited from it to barter their trade elsewhere; perhaps buying food produced by people they, in turn, will never know. The people who produced the food may, in turn, purchase their foreign machinery from America. And, the fascinating part of the whole cycle becomes clear when one realizes how probable it is that certain parts of this foreign machinery was manufactured here in the United States by a company who pays a salary to the original American who bought the pair of shoes! Thus, through a series of different worlds made up of people who may never know each other, each one impinges on the life of another so that the universal law of Action and Reaction, Cause and Effect, the cosmic Law of Karma is fulfilled.

The third interpretation of Karma comes from Edgar Cayce, the great "Sleeping Prophet," who through his enormous visionary qualities was able to help thousands of individuals find a healthier, more harmonious way of living. Nearly all of Cayce's work was based on the Law of Karma. Instead of expressing it as Buddha did, "You are what you think, having become what you thought", or as the mathematician Newton did, "For every action, there is an equal and opposite reaction", Cayce used two words to describe this fascinating cosmic law. He called it, "Meeting Self." What did he mean by this? How does one meet oneself? Was Cayce referring to a mirror through which each individual uses his life experiences and the people in them in order to see himself? What Cayce had discovered was that the best way to know man is to look at the way man looks at himself. The mirror does not lie, but shows what is truly there. Although it is not man's reality, it is a powerful enough reflection of his reality for him to believe that it is all that exists. Individuals love to know what others think of them. They seek approval and avoid disapproval from external sources. Thus, the external conditions in an individual's life are merely the mirrored reflection of all that springs forth from him internally.

Man constantly seeks to see himself through the eyes of others. Interestingly enough, the more he does this the less he is truly himself. But through habits of generations it seems to be the most natural way for man to learn; or to put it more clearly, for man to put himself into the illusion that he is learning. In the most normal, mundane, everyday conversations that people have with each other it is so easy to notice how individuals are almost always talking to themselves while giving the appearance of talking to another. There is always the outward verbal conversation accompanied by the inner conversation one is having with oneself at the same time, questioning constantly what the other individual is giving to them or taking from them, what they themselves are giving or taking, and how much approval they are receiving for their efforts. If an individual lives his life in this manner how difficult is it to know his Karma? If the friends he chooses are truthful, then he is sincerely concerned with meeting himself. If on the other hand, he has friends for convenience, who are more tactful than truthful, then he is not meeting himself. This is based on the fact that individuals tend to seek out support for the righteousness of their beliefs and behavior. Instead of privately looking in their own mirror, they tend to seek the mirrors that will reflect the facets of themselves that they are ready to see. Thus, when a married woman associates with many friends who are either divorced or single in greater numbers than those who are married, it becomes very easy to see the direction in which she is pointing herself. If the majority of a man's friends are successful individuals in business, rather than those who avoid responsibility, then it becomes easy to see the measures of success that the man is walking toward. If a child has many goal-oriented friends this, too, says much for the child. Thus in the process of meeting oneself, according to Edgar Cayce's definition of Karma, there is a very strong tendency for the old wives tale that "Birds of a feather flock together" to have a strong element of truth in it.

The definition of meeting oneself, however, does not end here. It is based on the fact that within each individual there are also actions and reactions. Only when the two balance each other is the person able to come together at the center of his being. Only then, does he truly meet himself.

According to Ouspensky, there are different selves within an individual, each one trying to hold momentary rulership over the others. He compares them to a ferris wheel, where one moment one self is on top and in control and then in another moment another self is on top trying to assume an equal amount of control. The perfect example is in the purchasing of an automobile, where the self in control at the moment impulsively decides to purchase on a time payment plan the desired object for which all the other selves will have to pay. But, the true self is none of these. Instead it is the center of the wheel; the one part of an individual that is able to view and ultimately understand all of the other divergent personalities that pull it in different directions at different times. Thus, in order to meet oneself according to Cayce, one must learn how to be at the center of one's wheel so that instead of looking at life through a series of experimental mirrors, one is able to emit the pure essence that comes from the best oneness he can achieve with his singular, divine, all-knowing being.

We see then, three different facets of the Karmic triangle. First, in the words of Buddha, "You are what you think having become what you thought." Second, from the mathematical laws of Sir Isaac Newton, "For every action (in your life) there will be (a time when you will experience) an equal and opposite reaction." And, thirdly, from the studies of Edgar Cayce, the process through which one meets oneself. In all three cases, Karma gives the appearance of the subtle workings of Yin and

Yang conflict. Thought is the precipitator of action. Action causes reaction. Through the process of action and reaction man is ultimately able to develop a Third higher self which is capable of viewing the constant battles between his Yin and Yang behavior from a much clearer vantage point. And, it is from this vantage point, the center of Ouspensky's ferris wheel, the very core at the essence of being, through which man can see the truth about himself. Only this kind of perception allows one to slowly absolve oneself from the laws of Karmic interaction.

The analogy of the pyramid or triangle is one of the oldest and most mystical known to man. The triangle has two points at the bottom and one at the top. Man has two legs, but one mind which, if he is to be unified, must rule the coordination of both. In all the teachings of Yoga there is always a reference made to how man in his lower self, divided by the Yin and Yang or positive and negative influences he sees in the world around him, fights with himself. First he is one, then he is the other. But only through learning and training does he develop the third part of himself, the top of the triangle which looks at the other two identities he has created through a cosmic viewpoint. Yoga calls this top point of the triangle *the impersonal I.* It is only through the development of this impersonal I, in its oneness of mind, that man is able to finally know himself. And, from this knowing eventually comes a fullness which is the product of actually having "met oneself," and even more important, accept oneself! This point at the top of the triangle cannot exist alone. It is the outpouring of years of struggle between the two opposing points at the bottom of the triangle.

For centuries Astrology has focused on the Yin and Yang quality in man's nature; the positive and negative effects of planetary energies, and the relationship between the two. It is easy to view the world as a multitude of positive and negative forces because there are differences between night and day, love and hate, concepts of right and wrong, ideas of good and evil, and a multitude of other dualities which are constantly showing themselves. But there is also a larger and more multi-faceted view of things which does not see duality as a plentitude of opposing forces. This view does not base itself in terms of positive and neagtive, good and evil, right and wrong, here and there, yesterday and tomorrow, and all of the other divisions into which one's perception of things can divert one from the truth. Instead, there is one perception, which although it sees the positive and negative dualities also sees as much value in the negative as it does in the positive. It does not value the future any more or less than the past. It does not see day over night nor night over day. The most controversial and startling thing about this viewpoint of perception is that it does not favor good over evil nor evil over good. Instead, all duality is viewed as two sides of a coin, both of which are necessary in order for the coin to be complete.

There is a very simple reason why most people never reach this viewpoint. As long as an individual preoccupies his mind with the problems of duality, he lives in an oppressed consciousness. The world is not allowing him to be all that he feels he could be. From moment to moment as he keeps switching identifications from the positive to the negative and back again, he seeks to find blame for all that opposes what he believes to be the path of fulfilling his desires. He will blame his childhood, his religion, his sex, his teachers, his job, his friends, and the society he lives in for keeping him within all of the restrictions which he believes are the causes of the conflicts he feels within himself. What he does not realize is that by viewing things this way, he is doing all he can to violate the three principles which basically make up the Law of Karma. He is creating disharmonious thoughts which keep him from being the kind of creator he wants to be. He complains about the effects of his thoughts, which puts him out of harmony with the second principle of Karma, or the law of Cause and Effect. And finally, by constantly trying to see himself through the eyes of others, he is doing all he can to avoid actually meeting himself in the true light of his Divine understanding. Why then does man continually do all that ultimately keeps him from being one with himself? The answer is not mystical at all, but in fact is so obviously simple that in humanity's quest for truth it often gets overlooked. If man had nothing to complain about, if he had no outer world problems to blame for stopping his progress, if he had all of his financial and survival needs provided for, what would he do with himself? It is much easier to be a cork floating on water, waiting for the external current to move one hither and yon and to blame these external currents for all hindrances to one's progress than to actually take the responsibility of becoming all that one could be.

When Shakespeare said, ''To be or not to be, that is the question'' the world hardly understood what he meant. This lack of understanding does not stop merely because one is a student of Astrology, which happens to be the first door to understanding. There is hardly a student of Astrology who at one time or another does not seek to place blame for the circumstances in his life on one or another aspect being triggered in his horoscope chart. Thus, the nature of man is such as to always try to seek some scapegoat outside of himself for what he is not willing to face as his own truth. This looking outside of the self for reasons, effects, and causes brings about what Shakespeare would have called a state of ''not being.'' But, the moment an individual decides that he wants ''to be,'' then he starts truly ''meeting (him)self'' as the cause and the effect, the leader and the follower, the source and the reflection. In essence, he starts to become his own keeper. And, it is at this point that he can begin to understand the real meaning of Karma, for truly the only thing in common with all of the events, circumstances, and people in his life is *Himself!*

# Chapter Two

# THE KARMA OF "THE NOW"

For eons the concept of Karma has always been associated with reincarnation. Through all of its definitions, it has somehow synthesized itself into an essence that constantly says that the current life is the harvest of all lives before it. In many ways, this is true. However, this view tends to make one overlook the fact that today is yesterday's tomorrow. We live in an ever-changing world where there is in fact so much present-life Karma going on at every moment that it is indeed easier for us to see the past than the present. It is easier for man to face backwards, looking at all he has already lived through—the thoughts he has accumulated from reading, and those assimilated from his environment to understand the pattern of his life, rather than to realize that he is always creating new patterns. All he thought yesterday will echo in his mind today. All he thinks and does today will echo in his mind tomorrow. In fact, the truly aware person understands that there are no days. There is only the moment of "The Now." But, in the reality of chronological time, one must ask the question, "How long is The Now?" Does it mean a day, an hour, a few minutes, or the average attention span of the conscious mind which has been measured to be approximately four seconds? From one individual to another the definition of the word "Now" differs greatly.

Consider a person going through days and weeks of actions which lead him on a divergent path away from reaching his desired goals. One day he realizes this, and looking back at how many times he has strayed from himself, he comes up with the statement, "Now look what I have done." In a way, the thought is contradictory. The word "Now" means the present. The phrase "I have done" means the past. For this individual, the conception of "The Now" is a blend of many weeks in the past, the moment of realization in the present, and within seconds after that, the surfacing of what actions he plans to take in his future. Here we ask the question—how long in the future is he directing his energies? Thus, the concept of "Now" for this person may well be a period of a year or years.

Consider the same individual at a different time in his day, saying to himself, "I am hungry." He has realized a need within himself only seconds before. He has allowed it to express itself spontaneously, and will undoubtedly act on that need within a very short period of time. In this instance, the concept of the "Now" is only a few minutes.

Later that day, this same individual receives his college diploma which he has looked forward to since his teenage years when life goals became impressed upon him. He has worked diligently for four years and now must deal with what the piece of paper will mean to him for the rest of his life. In this instance, the "Now" is expanded over a very long period of years. In fact, when he reviews in his mind those particular courses which came easy to him and those which were particularly difficult, he is, in fact, tapping those areas with which he was familiar in former incarnations and those areas which are new experiences for him in the present life. Thus, we see many different levels operating at the same time. The idea of "Now" is an ever-changing reality; different for different individuals and constantly different for the same individual.

Because of this, it is easy to see how a person lives in all time at the same time. And, this is where an individual's confusion arises. He values that which lasts for moments. He values that which lasts for weeks or months. And, he values that which is everlasting. Constantly he is weighing the importance of these different "Nows" so that he can balance himself in each present moment.

Some individuals live a life dedicating themselves towards something that will outlive them. Thus, their primary concept of the "Now" is a time which they will never live to see. On the other end of the spectrum there are individuals who live only for the present moment, not caring about the future effects of their present actions. Within the same individual we find subtleties of thought and behavior patterns which lean toward one extreme and the other at the same time. These are the things which make people feel like hypocrites to themselves. Ultimately they question what life is all about, and what it is, if anything that they truly stand for.

When man lives only for the moment, the wider "Nows" which exist for years or thousands of years not only seem to catch up with him, but have a very strong power over his rising and falling tide of life. At the same time when man tries to live a very wide "Now" consisting of many years in the past and many years in the future, he tends to miss the spontaneity of singular moments in between. Thus, in the first instance, man is always overdoing, overexaggerating, and overemphasizing the power of each moment because it is all he can see. In the second instance he is underdoing, and underemphasizing his present moment, missing the vividness of life that is offered to him because he does not see the importance of the fleeting moment within the grand scheme of the wide "Now" he is perceiving.

The entire idea of time is based on perception. The

qualities of patience and impatience come from the kind of
"Now" that an individual sees. The question then arises,
which concept of "Now" is more important? And this
question becomes particularly significant for the individual who is able to see all of these different "Nows" at the
same time. Interestingly enough, there seems to be a very
well-defined pattern as to how these "Nows" work. Many
Gurus have taken several years out of their lives in order to
do their past incarnation Karma before settling themselves
into whatever mission they were to perform in the present
life. At the other end of the spectrum is the individual who
is not even aware that past incarnations exist, let alone that
they may have an influence on the present life. Talk to him
for a while. Observe his life and you will notice that for
moments, days, or even years on end, parts of him seem to
be "out to lunch." He is not all here, but rather forces
whose existence he denies are constantly pulling him to
times and places from his past. The more this occurs, the
more he loses his sense of presence in the focused moment
of the "Now." An individual may live beyond his means,
or within them. But, unless he knows what his means are,
he truly has no reference point from which to know *when*
he is doing *what*.

Since means have a lot to do with ends, an
individual must know his ends if his means are going to
meet them. But here, too, man confuses himself. Some
ends are goals of a lifetime, which take a lifetime to reach.
Some ends are fleeting moments whose rewards are less
gratifying. And some ends come from motivations started
in prior lifetimes. Thus, when we talk about goals, means
and ends we are again confronted with the concept of
man's perception of time. There is a great secret to time
that most of the human race is not aware of. Time is
usually thought of as a linear dimension moving
progressively forward, like a straight line moving from left
to right, or whatever direction one may choose. It

progresses by minutes, hours, days, weeks, and centuries, chronologically, giving the appearance of moving in a singular direction. Direction is what gives man a sense of proportion. It's interesting to note here, that the individual without purpose or direction seems to have all the time in the world, while the individual with much purpose and direction seems to have no time at all. What is the difference then, between all the time, and no time? We've often heard the expression, "there is no time like the present." There is a much deeper significance to this statement than what appears on the surface.

Take a piece of paper and fold it in half. Now on the left hand side of the paper, using some writing implement that easily rubs off (like charcoal, chalk, or heavy pencil) scribble a wavy horizontal line from the left side of the page up to the center crease. The waves don't have to be even. In fact, you will understand the entire concept of time and Karma much better if they aren't. When you've done this, fold the page at the crease, rubbing the piece of paper so that the wavy line you have made on the left side rubs off onto the right side of the page. Now open the page and observe the wavy line moving all the way across the paper. Notice how one side is the exact mirror image of the other. The crease at the center of the sheet of paper is exactly where man stands at any given point in time. It is, in fact, the reality of his "Now" experience. The left hand side of the page represents his past; the right hand side, his future. Can you see from this example why it has always been so easy for fortune tellers to predict one's future? What they have always done was in fact, look at the reflection or the mirror image of an individual's past. The astute fortune teller, being able to pin the person into their own individual "Now" and knowing the power that people give their past, over their future, simply sees the individual's past, measures where the individual is now and is then able to tell by looking at the right hand side of the sheet of paper, or the mirror image of the past, a very accurate outline of what the person's future will be like. Peaks and valleys in the wavy line on the left side of the page can be measured in inches which can be equated to weeks, months, or years. Similar occurrences can be predicted, sometimes even to the date, by measuring the same number of inches and equating them to days, months, or years on the right side of the page. It is quite an unfortunate fact that most people who visit fortune tellers spend their future repeating their past. The more a person holds onto memories, either good or bad, the more predictable his future is, because truly it is not in his own hands, but in the reflection of his memories on the opposite side of the piece of paper.

There is great distance in the wavy line on the left side of the sheet of paper, symbolizing the past. There is also great distance in its future reflection, symbolized by the wavy line on the right side of the piece of paper. But, the dot at the center of the line formed by the crease has no direction in time. It does not extend to the future or from the past. The most amazing fact is that when the piece of paper is folded, the past and future mirror each other but the dot at the center does not recreate itself in either the past or the future. This is the point in time that represents the focused field of the "Now" experience.

It is the center of awareness of both past and future, along with the realization that only the "Now" exists. Going back to our earlier analogy of the individual who tries to live in all time as compared to the individual who lives for the present only, we must consider one more factor to make the picture clear. It would seem that the individual who is living in the present only is living in the "Now." But, this is not necessarily the case! To see this, take the sheet of paper and fold it again so that a crease appears half an inch or so to the right of the original crease. Open the paper and look at it. You are confronted with a second "Now" to deal with. If you were to fold the paper again, there would be a third "Now" and so on. But none of these represent the "Now" I am speaking about. They are created because of the powerful tendency of the past to mirror itself in the future. And, they are reflected in the life of an individual who lives a sequence of Now moments without being truly in touch with that one dot at the center of the sheet of paper, which is the only real "Now" experience.

It has been said that everything changes, but nothing changes. The law of Cause and Effect, in essence the very foundation of Karma, is rooted very strongly in the meaning of this phrase. For some, life is a series of changes leading to no change. For others, life is a series of changes leading to great change. For still others, the patterns of events in life never seem to change at all. The true "Now" at the center of the sheet of paper sees the changes in the past and the future and changes constantly within itself. But, although it is changing constantly it never moves from the center of the sheet of paper. And, in that sense, on a much deeper level, it does not change.

If man is constantly vibrating to the echoes of his past while projecting himself to the promise of the future, he keeps moving that point on the piece of paper from left to right. Every time he moves the point to the left, he draws from his past. Then, according to the law of equal and opposite reaction, he will move that point to the future which will then recreate his past. This is how man lives in a Karmic condition. His past has been a series of failures and successes. And, the moment he thinks about it, it is automatic for him to project the same thoughts into his future.

It is extremely difficult for even five minutes to pass without someone experiencing several thoughts of his past. He does this because it offers him security in the future. It makes him feel that he has some control over what will later occur in his life. What he doesn't realize is that constantly jumping from past to future drains his energies enormously. He lives in a lethargic state of limbo where constant actions and reactions govern his every moment. Thus, he never quite realizes the potential that God had intended for him. He lives in a world of illusion, believing that he is going somewhere along his linear conception of time, through which (according to his own set of values) he measures his progress.

For many, it is a frightening experience to attempt to live in the "Now", because it means that the individual is no longer holding onto his past or worried about his future. It is interesting to note that the pattern followed by those people who have been able to reach living in the "Now" has always been similar. The individual who is constantly projecting his life into the future by setting out to change the world for the better, ultimately will be very disappointed when he finds out that it is good enough. And in fact, the discovery he will make is that all is as it should be. The individual who constantly dwells on past injustices he has suffered will ultimately realize that he cannot change the world of the past. When Buddha sat under the tree of knowledge for twenty-nine days seeking the greatest answer to life, he was finally brought to understand that the key of life is "to be." By projecting one's energies towards the future or the past, one loses his sense of being in the present. The present "Now" is the moment you are reading this sentence, and the more you reflect upon how it may in the future correct mistakes you have made in the past, the less you are getting in touch with the "Now" of this sentence. Individuals who are trying to elevate their past Karma through overcoming long established habit patterns all manage to do it the same way. The alcoholic who is overcoming his habit prays, "Lord help me make it through the day." The cigarette smoker who is trying to cut down on his consumption uses the same method. In fact, the focus of the "Now" may be narrowed down to a day or an hour or a few minutes until the individual is able to center himself in the harmony of his "Now" experience. The path of every individual who has ever mastered himself has always been through the realization that too much past or too much future leaves too little creative energy for full expression in the "Now."

Perhaps one of the best ways of understanding what the "Now" is can be seen by the attitude of a writer when he is in harmony with himself. The joy he experiences is during the writing when he is actually participating in the creative process. The joy of the reader comes at a later date when through his reading, he is participating in the creative process. When at some still future date, readers compliment the writer on a job well done, the writer is left with little to say, for it is not part of his "Now" experience.

To consider another example, think of the individual with apprehensions about the future coupled with enough regrets from the past that he cannot see the present at all. Consider further, a student of Astrology waiting for a particular transit to make the events in his life better, while, until that transit occurs, he creates an imbalance in the rest of his being by not making use of all the other energies he has available to him in the now.

In order to live in the "Now" one must become acquainted with the fact that there is "no time" except that which one is able to make use of. Questions and problems whose solutions the individual is seeking in the future tend to push him into a conception of time that he cannot yet make use of. It does not exist. And that is why all his pondering cannot bring him the answer he is seeking, because the more he ponders the more he leaves the "Now." There are individuals who suffer from states of depression which stem from rejections or failures in the past which does not now exist, or from beliefs that they cannot meet their own expectations in the future which also does not exist. One startling thing about depression is that everytime the individual has the opportunity to talk to another person, he seems to lift out of his depressed state, only to return to it at a later time. What is really happening is that while he is receiving the acceptance of a listener, he is experiencing the "Now," and the moment he no longer has a listener he quickly slips back into past problems that he cannot solve. It is much like the individual who wants to make a bank deposit on Sunday, when the banks are closed. His desire for action will fail because he is not coping with the "Now," but instead he is trying to force open the bank doors which will open by themselves a day later. The individual who spends an entire week planning to mow his lawn on Saturday not only misses the "Now" of each day he is living until then, but what does he do on Saturday when it rains? All of these cases show how easy it is to *not* take life one day at a time. By living one day at a time, life becomes much simpler and much more effortless than by complicating it with problems that do not exist in the present.

Living one day at a time, as difficult as it may seem, is only the first step toward approaching the "Now". The second step is for the individual to understand how much of the day he is trying to live at the same time. If, in the morning, he is thinking about his afternoon, and in the afternoon he is thinking about his evening and his morning, and in his evening he is thinking about the time preceding it along with what he will do the following day, he is truly not living in the "Now." Although he has narrowed his perception to approximately a twenty-four hour interval, he can frustrate himself constantly by living either ahead or behind himself rather than functioning to his best ability in each moment. By considering what one will do next, the fullness of joy that the present moment can hold is dissipated. The individual's sense of presence becomes dulled as he loosely allows himself to spill over into time that does not now exist. A musician practicing his instrument does best when his entire attention, coordination, and his whole being is focused on the particular note he is playing at the moment. He is one with his instrument. However, the moment his mind wanders to how his notes are being perceived by his listeners, he is losing the "Now"; for by doing this he is actually creating a time lag and if he perceives any negative feedback from his listeners, he loses his oneness with his instrument and starts to make errors. It is much like the ballplayer pitching a perfect game until he realizes that fifty thousand people are watching him. Then he begins to perceive himself through fifty thousand different "Nows" instead of his own, creating a very strong likelihood that he will make an error as a result of losing touch with himself. This leads us to still another definition of the "Now," and that is based on how an individual perceives the "Here."

We live in a very big world with many things occurring in many places all the time. Newspapers and mass media direct our attention to all parts of the globe every day. Loud noises in the streets screech in our ears and pull our attention away from our presence of self. In the same way as there is only one "Now," there is also only one "Here." The "Here" is the center of where an individual is in consciousness, right "Now." If one works to master the secret of time but cannot master the "Here" then he is still missing a very large portion of the "Now."

The mind is a funny thing. Through imagination it likes to wander to different places all the time. Consider an individual thinking of a loved one far away. Consider another individual in the course of his daily work, imagining where he will spend his vacation. Consider still another individual thinking of going shopping and questioning which store will have the greatest sales. In all ᵗᴸ ᵤₒᵤ instances, the mind wanders to different places, taking away from the spontaneity of the present moment. People have a peculiar tendeᵤᵤᵧ to watch over people. They travel through mailboxes, holding oᵤₜc their letters until they are assured that the letters reach theiᵣ destination. They travel through telephone lines lingering in other people's minds until they are sure that whatever they have verbalized has been accepted. Can you imagine how many people, things, places, and ideas are capable of jamming an individual's mind at any given moment? These are the reasons why most people are so thoroughly exhausted at the end of each day: they try to put too many times and places into each moment.

The "Now" is the time you are in at this moment. But, it is also confined to the place you are in at this moment. If you are painting a picture, the "Now" is the particular brushstroke you are painting at this moment. Observations of most great accomplished artists and musicians show that they are completely oblivious to everything outside of what they are doing. Regardless of what work, play, chores or duty an individual is involved with, his "Now" is his focused involvement in the moment. But, it is also important that he realize that his "here" is accomplished by not trying to live through others, but rather by staying within himself which is the only real source of anything that can ever emanate from him.

There is a very strong tendency for most people to live their lives through others, always secretly questioning the balance of how much they are giving and receiving in every relationship. They hold on to other people's dreams and therefore must live in other people's places violating their own sense of the "Here."

Think of the world as a giant ocean, with each person being a single droplet of water. How tiny and insignificant we are; and yet, within each droplet of water is a model for the entire ocean. A droplet of water does not have to be in another place or another time other than exactly where it is. Instead, it is able to harmoniously blend with the current all around it in the moment of the "Now." Even individuals who live in the "Now" and therefore dissipate less energy—as a result of which they achieve great things—lose their sense of "Now" every time they look back at their achievements.

Whatever exists in one's thoughts that cannot be dealt with in the exact time and place that the individual is in are only distractions from his "Now" reality. The object of life is not only to evolve the Soul, but to be happy in the process. Thus, the journey through Karma is equally as important as the destination.

Whether an individual studies Astrology or not, he will still reap the Yin and Yang effects of his thoughts and deeds in prior incarnations. There is no question that to some extent man creates, and meets the effects of all he creates, in the current life as well. But, the moment he stands and loudly claps his hands, he is experiencing the pure essence of the "Now".

All of the Zen principles are aimed at teaching an individual how to experience the "Now" because it is the only way for a person to stop repowering his past, bringing it into the present, complaining about it, and therefore, continuing his sympathetic vibration of echoes of what no longer is. The more an individual perpetuates memories of his past the more it becomes his present. And, the more he does this, the more he is missing the actual essence of the "Now" experience.

Whether man feels good or bad about himself, due to past Karmic circumstances, he has a tremendous tendency to measure his goodness against his concept of God as formulated by others either hundreds or thousands of years ago. This prevents him from realizing the "living God" in the "Now"; the omnipresent giving and forgiving God who does not care what man has done thousands of years ago as much as what he is doing now.

Astrology is a language. It is one of the many ways for man to see God. The problem has always been that too much of the human race views God as a force external to themselves. As a result of this, they seek God in things, circumstances, people and events outside of themselves. When they do this, they leave their center of being and lose the pure essence of the Here and Now—the very vivid reality that the God within them is prompting them to experience.

One of the greatest services that Astrology has done has been to break down the barriers between different religions. Astrology teaches that an individual, regardless of his religion, sex or creed, is very much his horoscope chart. At the same time, one of the great disservices that Astrology has done is to further the myth that God is outside of the individual. Even spiritual Astrologers "preach" that one should use his Astrology chart to aspire in the direction of evolution. Here man gets confronted with spiritual ego, which is no less distracting from his true essence than his personal ego. The process of evolution is a natural one. With or without desire, with or without aspiration, a sapling will grow into a tree. But whether the sapling has desire or not (if indeed it could) it will become a tree in its proper season. A child will grow up when it is ready to, regardless of whether individuals try to speed up or hamper the process. The important thing here is that the beauty of the sapling or the tree, the child or the adult is not in what it will one day become—for that is a time that does not yet exist—but rather in the function, essence of presence, and fullness of whatever measure it is expressing in the moment of the "Now."

It is to this point that Astrology must begin to focus its attention if, as a race and as a universe, we are to come together in the eternal oneness that exists and of which we only have glimpses in rare moments.

# Chapter Three

# THE HOROSCOPE AND "THE NOW"

The horoscope is made up of four basic factors—the planets, the signs, the aspects, and the houses. To understand these properly, one must be able to clearly distinguish the differences between the four. The planets symbolize energies. The constellations in which they reside color these energies much like filters in front of pure white movie spotlights which change the color into a particular ray of light before it hits the stage. Thus, knowing the kind of energy that a planet emits, the sign in which it falls will, in subtle ways, shade that energy to its own coloring. The aspects, or relationships between planets, and the signs they fall in, may be compared to a series of movie lights of different colors, placed in different corners of the theater, but all focused on the stage of players. The houses which symbolize life experiences, external to the true inner self, created by Karma (very much the result of the use of self-will), can be likened to a revolving stage upon which all activity is acted out.

If one is to question which of the four astrological factors (the planets, signs, houses, or aspects) is closest to the true nature of the individual then one must realize that the theater lights, their colors, their location in the theater and the revolving stage upon which they shine each have a different effect on the actor, but are not, in themselves, the actor. Thus, while the planets shed light, the signs they are in color these lights; the aspects between the planets show the various blendings, shadings and combinations of lights which will reach the actor; and the stage shows the setting within whose framework the actor will function. None of these speak of the play that the actor will enact—for that comes in part from his own choosing, but is very much Karmically rooted. What is most interesting is the fact that, depending upon which play the actor will act out, the setting on his stage must be different accordingly. It is for this reason that the astrological houses (as symbolized by the setting of life's experiences) must be viewed as that which is external or outside of the real self; for there is no question that God has given man the will and the power to choose the life experiences he will enact. Even if one considers many actions the result of past actions, one cannot ignore the fact that, at some time in the past, choices based on free will began a particular Karmic pathway. In the present, too, Karmic doors are constantly closing or opening depending upon the free will choices that an individual makes. Even after an individual has made his choices in terms of what kind of experiences he would like to be a part of, he still possesses a very human quality which gives him a wide latitude of expression. Thus, whatever script an individual is playing, he will make use of the movie lights and their different colors (the planets and the signs) for they magnify his expression and give him the power and the color of his output. The setting, or houses, give him a frame of reference outside of himself so that he can see and feel an external feedback which helps to convince him that his actions are appropriate. The actor on the stage tries to become part of his setting and blend with it so that his act is convincing to still another factor—his ever changing audience, which may be compared to the transiting planets which from day to day, week to week and year to year constantly give him different external impressions of his natal chart. This is very much like the changing faces of his audiences to life, whose own desires and needs he is constantly trying to please.

Still, God never asks man to be an actor—only "to be." Many poets and musicians of deep sensitivities have observed how easy it is for man to live outside of himself; how distractions make it difficult for him to live his own existence. This was expressed very aptly in a song by James Taylor which said, "We are riding on a railroad, singing someone else's song." The point is that if man is truly to meet himself, he must stop looking at himself through the eyes of others. He must throw away the mirror and, like two candles burning into one, he must allow the excess wax of past impressions to melt away. Man must stop wasting all the energies he has through the eyes and experiences of others who are constantly trying to do the same thing. Only when this is done can a person truly become one with himself.

Towards this end, I have devised a new method of laying out the horoscope chart.* Its goal is to allow both the student and Astrologer to see things as they really are rather than as impressionistic symbols implying a distorted reality. In the old method, a 360 degree circle was divided into twelve equal parts, with the houses shown inside of the circle. A second circle appeared outside of this, and given its own divisions, depicted the twelve zodiac signs. The planets were placed within the houses, not within the signs. Still, it would be obvious which signs they appeared in, because of how one circle lined up with the other. In my new method, this entire system is reversed. The houses appear in the outer circle while the signs appear in the inner circle. The planets are still placed in the inner circle and are

---

* Similar to an invention of Margaret Hone.

graphically shown in the signs in which they fall, rather than in the houses. The ultimate reason for drawing a chart this way is to see reality more closely to the way it truly is.

The following charts are of the exact same birthday, time and place. Chart A is drawn according to the old method where the houses appear in the inner circle. Chart B is the new method showing the signs in the inner circle. Both charts are using Placidus Cusps.

The first fallacy with the old method is very apparent. Notice that the horoscope blank has divided the 360 degrees of the zodiac into twelve equal thirty degree sections of the pie. In chart A this is very misleading. Since we are dealing with an unequal house system and each house is visually drawn to be the exact same size, interpretation becomes difficult. The individual reading the chart is visually led to believe that which is not. Thus, he must mentally deceive what his eyes are telling him in order to understand the truth of what he is looking at. It is very common for charts to appear with very large and very small houses. Yet, in the method depicted by chart A, this is not shown. The student must go through some arithmetical gymnastics in order to conceive of the differences in house sizes. Now look at chart B. Here the inner circle is being used to show the twelve zodiac signs. Visually, and you can measure it with a protractor, each sign appears as a thirty degree section of the pie. This is exactly as it should be since each constellation in the heavens has been divided into thirty degree sections. The outer circle which depicts the houses shows each house division as the actual size that it is. Visually, smaller houses appear smaller, and larger houses appear larger. As a result there are no mental gymnastics to go through in order to see the correct perspective between the twelve equal zodiac signs and the exact sizes of the twelve unequal houses.

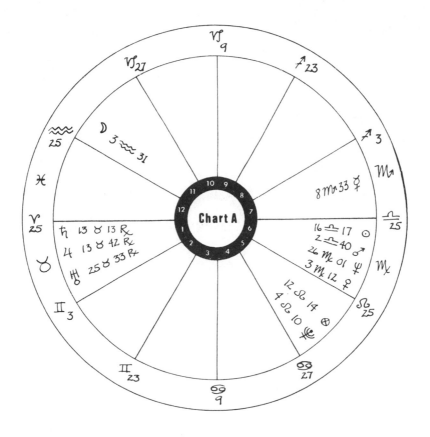

John Lennon
October 9, 1940
Manchester, England

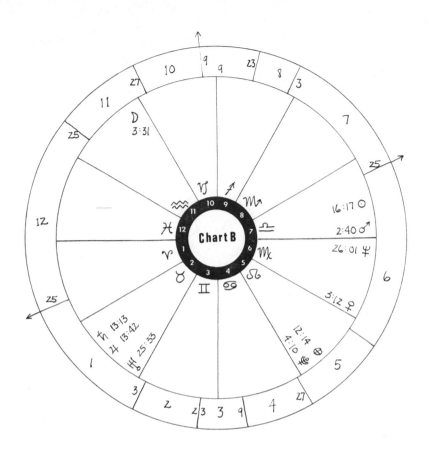

John Lennon
October 9, 1940
Manchester, England

If there were no other reason to employ this method of charting, this alone would be enough but there are other reasons. The second reason is based on a matter of simplicity. Notice that in chart A each planetary symbol must have the zodiac sign drawn next to it. Thus, each zodiac sign is drawn twice—first in the outer circle in order to show the sign and then again with every planet in that sign. Now look at chart B. Here each zodiac sign is drawn only once. Because the signs are placed on the inner part of the circle, and the planets appear within these thirty degree segments, each planet need not have the sign written next to it. Thus, drawing the planetary symbol within the thirty degree section of the pie that it falls in, coveniently shows the sign that the planet is in without having to go through the double work of writing it again.

The third reason has to do with intercepted signs. Notice in chart A there are two signs missing (Taurus and Scorpio) giving an incomplete impression of the zodiac. These signs are not missing from the zodiac. The constellation belt follows in sequence, without any signs being left out. By putting the signs in the inner circle in chart B, each sign of the zodiac is represented. In this way, the confusion involved in looking at intercepted signs does not arise.

The fourth reason is based on the ease with which one may visually interpret aspects rather than having to constantly count off the amount of degree numbers between planets in a chart which is visually misleading. We know that the fixed signs, if connected to each other, should appear to form a Grand Cross. The same is true of the Cardinal and Mutable signs. Notice that in chart A, the fixed sign Taurus appears to be forming almost a quincunx with the next fixed sign Leo. In turn Leo appears to be forming almost a sextile with the next fixed sign, Scorpio. Scorpio appears to be forming something between a trine and a quincunx with the next fixed sign,

Aquarius. Thus, if the fixed signs were connected in chart
A, the Grand Cross that they actually form would appear
completely distorted to the eye. Now look at chart B.
Without even using a mathematical protractor, it is
visually obvious that each fixed sign is forming an exact
ninety degree square to the next one; and that the four
together are forming a perfectly-symmetrical Cross. This
makes aspect interpretation much simpler.

Find the aspect between Saturn and Pluto in Chart
A. If you use a protractor (which measures exact angles),
these two planets appear to be between 130 to 140 degrees
apart. In chart B, the square which is less than nine degrees
from being exact, measures out to be almost the exact ninety
degrees that it practically is. In fact, if you use a protractor,
measuring the aspect between Saturn and the Part of
Fortune from Chart A to Chart B, this difference between
proper and improper graphic representation becomes even
more pronounced. In order to count off aspects according
to the old method, one must first accept the fact that the
symbolic planetary placements on the chart pad, do not in
any way represent where the planets truly are. Then, one
must know the exact order of signs and very often one must
count off the degrees and intercepted signs in order to find
the exact distance between planets. This makes the drawing
of aspects a very tedious and cumbersome process, with the
end result being a visual misrepresentation of their
relationship to each other.

To find the aspect between Saturn and Pluto or
Saturn and the Part of Fortune in chart B, all one has to
do is put one's finger on the Saturn symbol at thirteen
degrees thirteen minutes of Taurus (Retrograde) and then
move to thirteen degrees thirteen minutes Gemini (which is
the next sign) which completes thirty degrees. Move again
to thirteen degrees thirteen minutes of Cancer (which is the
next succeeding sign) and you have completed sixty
degrees. Move once more to thirteen degrees, thirteen
minutes of Leo. That completes ninety degrees. Then see if

the Part of Fortune and Pluto are within the nine degree allotted orb of thirteen degrees thirteen minutes Leo. They are, and the chart now visually shows two squares. To illustrate this further, consider the distance between Pluto and Mercury. In chart A, they appear to be forming an approximate sextile, but in chart B they show up as the square that they actually are. Perhaps the best observation of all can be made from the fact that both charts contain a fixed cross between the planets, Pluto, Mercury, the Moon, Saturn and Jupiter (I am allowing a slightly larger orb here between the Moon and Jupiter because of Jupiter's width of effect and the fact that the Moon is one of the luminaries). Nevertheless, if you draw the fixed cross in chart A, it will appear lopsided enough for you not to see it as a fixed cross. In chart B, however, the fixed cross is clearly observable.

Along these same lines of aspect interpretation, the old method of charting presents still another difficulty. This difficulty shows itself most in the ability to see stelliums and conjunctions as they truly are. In chart A there is a four planet stellium in the Sixth house. If one does not look closely at the exact degree numbers, the planets appear to be forming a giant conjunction. In fact only Mars and Neptune are part of that conjunction. One side of the conjunction shows Venus out of orb from Neptune. And, on the other side, the Sun is out of orb from Mars. Thus, what first appears to be a very large conjunction is actually only a four planet emphasis in the Sixth house. Now look at these same four planets in chart B. Notice the Mars, Neptune conjunction visually appearing to be the conjunction that it is, while Venus and the Sun are distanced properly so that one does not make the mistake of interpreting these four planets together. Still, they all appear in the Sixth house as they should.

Observing a transit according to the old method as depicted in Chart A, it would seem to be having an effect on all four planets during a relatively short period of time.

In chart B, however, the separation between these planets makes it easier to visualize the approximate length of time it will take for a transiting planet to move from one natal planet to the next. In addition to this, chart B makes it easier to see the aspects that transits are forming with each other. Transits in opposition, square or trine to each other will appear exactly as they are in the new method. In the old method, the relationship between transits was as difficult to see as the aspect relationships between natal planets.

All of these reasons would be enough to realize why chart B shows a more easily readable and accurate description of what really is than chart A. But there is a fifth, and more important, reason for using this new method than I have mentioned so far and it has to do with an individual's experiences, his Karma, his perception of himself and the universe around him. When the houses are placed on the outside of the zodiac wheel rather than on the inside, they are symbolically showing twelve areas of life experience which are truly external to one's real self. In the old method of charting, where the houses appear in the inner circle, it almost leads one to believe that one is a total product of one's experiences rather than the fact that an individual has free will within his Soul to choose his experiences. It is through the outer world that he sees the changes and colors and movement around him, but much like the painter with his palette, he is free to dip his brush, mix or blend any of the colors available to him in order to lead his own personal creative life. The painting which is the end result does not come from the different colors on his palette at all; they are only useful tools for him to express what was inside him all the time. This can be demonstrated in a very interesting way. Time and time again we see individuals who have experienced transits through certain houses of their horoscope and from our knowledge of Astrology we have expected certain kinds of occurrences under these conditions, yet the individual did not experience what we expected. This occurs often enough to leave the Astrologer befuddled—ultimately coming to the conclusion that the astrological effect of the transit was correct, but that the individual was too out of tune with the universe to notice it. Consider the converse of this thought. Is it possible that something in such individuals recognizes an inner power within the self that actually transcends the winds of change in the external environment?

It becomes increasingly clear that each man is the center of his own universe. And, the more he responds and reacts to forces outside of himself, the more he loses himself in the changing universes of others. There is no question that the planets exert strong forces. But, if a man is reading a book and temporarily loses his train of thought because he is distracted by the sound of a car passing in the street, which is so much closer to him than the planets, then we must consider a new way of understanding planetary energies and the entire body of Astrology. By doing this, we can gain a new perspective which will make Astrology a better tool through which man can grow.

Man has the choice of either being himself or his environment. The planets, signs, aspects and houses symbolize the environment of the play he has chosen to act. If an individual decides to wait for years for a particular transit to bring him benefit, what is he doing with the rest of his horoscope in the meantime? Is it acting on him, or is he learning how to harmonize the energies it represents so that he can fulfill to his best potential, the here and "Now"?

Most of mankind is "asleep" most of the time. Every time a person is not using the potential in his chart, his chart is using him!

Man must be his own producer. God has given him the gift. From within him will emanate that part of God that he can express. If man waits for the universe to impress itself on him, then he not only loses his "Now" but becomes a mere fraction of the fullness and richness that was intended for him.

Astrology is a language. It is one of the ways in which man can learn to gather his forces so that he does not have to blame outside occurrences and people for his failure to be all that he can be. Too often we find people living in each other's shadows, becoming appendages of each other's egos for fear of finding out who they really are. And yet, it is only through self-discovery, void of all the subterfuges that mask it, that an individual gains the opportunity to experience the vivid "Now" quality of his existence.

We do not have Karma with others, only with ourselves. We do not have Karma with time, only in the way we use time. We do not have Karma with space, only in the way we use space. A man's life stands or falls on his perception and use of his "Now." It is all he has. If he is unable to use his own now, then he tries to use others. He lives outside of himself and may, in fact, bring happiness to others, but he will never sample the full happiness within himself. Astrology's highest purpose, then, is to help each individual understand his own "Now."

There is Karma in the "Now" but it is also created and resolved in the "Now." This occurs thousands of times daily as an individual has a thought and answers his own thought. In effect, he becomes the Law of Cause and Effect within himself. He is the actor and the audience, the creator and the observor to the lights, the coloring and the setting. He is, in fact, the "Now," for in reality he is all that is happening. In order for an individual to understand this, he must confront one very basic universal fact. *Either man understands the nature of the planets and learns how to act through their energies accordingly in the "Now" or he is used by the planets to be everything but the perfect actor at the center of his life.*

# Chapter Four

# THE LUMINARIES AND "THE NOW"

## THE SUN AND THE NOW

The Sun symbolizes the pure essence of life. It is the radiating force that gives light and vitality to everything in our universe. The Sun is the light of your life, and the sign it falls in is the very specific color of your life expression. It is the very essence of presence itself including your strength, your power, and the richness of your being in the "Now" moment. Because the Sun holds rulership over the sign Leo, one of whose qualities is admiration, there is a very powerful tendency for individuals to admire and seek the sunshine that they see in other people's lives. Thus, a person seeks to better himself by learning how to use the disciplines of Capricorn through Capricorns he knows. He tries to learn the fairness of Libra through Librans he is acquainted with. Through this pattern of bettering oneself through admiration of the finer qualities he sees in others, he may one day attain those qualities. However, when and if he does, he will have lost his own "Now," for instead of being the Sun of his own existence, he will have become parts of his external environment, finding himself removed from the pure essence of all he really is.

The Sun is the solar self. It is that part of an individual around which all else revolves. It is his vital life

force—and the warmth he experiences by being in tune
with his own vibration. In order to do this, he must
understand that it is his Sun that is encouraging him to
shine in the brilliance of his own "Now." Whoever he was
a moment ago, he no longer is. The Sun will shine
tomorrow, but that is not here yet. Thus, at any given
moment he can experience the full brilliance of his being
by simply being himself.

The Sun gives one power, will and energy to create
in the "Here" and "Now." If an individual thinks or lives
in too many yesterdays or tomorrows, he dissipates his
power, losing the vivid presence of the "Now" moment.

A student called me on the telephone and asked me
what I was doing. My reply was, "I am talking to you."
This is the solar presence of the "Now." Nothing else
exists except the full brilliance that an individual can
express.

The Sun radiates, but does not reflect. The
brilliance of being in the "Now" comes through radiating
all that one can without reflecting upon past or future
actions which only disperse the full power of one's Sun
sign. The Sun, says, "I am here, I am now," or in Jesus'
own words, "I am that I am." There is no doubt or
question in the expression of the "Now" through the
Sun's energy; for doubts and questions stem from man's
conceptions of past and future. The more man reflects
about himself, his environment, and his circumstances, the
less he is able to experience the full solar power of his
"Now." He is—and he is enough for himself. The
moment an individual begins to realize how much solar
power he truly has, he automatically realizes how easily he
has been dissipating his energies.

The Sun symbolizes the happiness and the joy of
man's creative instinct. It is the expression of his will. But,
far too often individuals try to impress their will on others.
By doing this, an individual takes himself away from

himself, dispersing his energies on what is not the "Here."
The desire to will things does the same, for it takes a
person away from the "Now." When a person starts to get
in touch with his solar power he discovers an unfailing
source of supply and support. The dullness in life melts
away and is replaced by the vital energy which creates the
vivid "Now" reality.

No zodiac sign is really better or worse than any
other. They are just different ways of experiencing the
"Now." There is much to be said for one's solar energy,
from whose roots can come a joyous acceptance of all one
is. "Now" is now. The "Now" of the Sun is who I am by
what I am without questioning the correctness of my
reflection.

The Sun radiates because it does. The fact that it
happens to light up the other planets in the process is
merely incidental. And, it does not move from one planet
to the next asking for feedback of how well it is doing.
Instead it is doing the only thing it knows how to do. And
it is, therefore, doing it in the best way that it knows.

"Now" is the moment; the mos. opportune time
and place in which the self can be. We've all heard the
expression—"Today is the first day of the rest of your
life." If one is to live in the "Now" of their Sun, this
statement is not exactly true. It should be "Today is all
there is." The very fact that some individuals realize this
while others do not separates the brilliant, vivid creators of
life, from the dull, drab existence of the dreamers. In order
to understand how the Sun can help one be in the "Now,"
it is not enough to build aspirations along positive
directions focused along pathways leading towards all one
can be, for as positive as such thoughts may seem, all they
do is remove a person from his "Now," projecting him
into a future which is uncertain. The strength and power of
the solar "Now" comes from the awareness that it is all
that exists! When this realization is reached, a great

oneness occurs within the self, and the constant battle stemming from the admiration of others, finally ceases. The individual realizes that he is—all he is! The "Now" of your Sun, is saying to you, "Don't tell me about all you can be." "Be it now!" And, as you are being it, again, don't think about it for you will lose your state of being by accepting the admiration which is a reflection of your state of being in place of your true state of being.

The Sun is an unbelievable source of power and magnetism. It can purify an individual's entire life if he is willing to learn how to unite with his own presence. Every time he asks others how he is doing, he muddies his presence with theirs, losing in great measure his total power of being in the "Now."

There is Karma in the "Now," but it is resolved instantaneously as the speed of the solar light governs man's actions and reactions within himself blending both into a vivid current presence that is the true expression of his Divine being.

There is no person who has not at one time or another sat down and pondered, perhaps for years on end, the question of who he is. Perplexed and confused, the maze of thoughts and actions and reflections continues until the individual reaches the "Sunlight of his day." Whatever path, religion or attitude an individual follows, if he is to reach truth, he must ultimately come to the realization of complete unity with his Sun sign. When he does this, his years of struggle and strife will be reduced to three simple words—"I am Now." And, from that day forward, his life takes on a different nuance. Each day is a new beginning, for in every moment, he is in touch with his present and in contact with his place. The objects around him begin to dance and sing and move in the "Now" that he has become a part of.

People constantly seek to better themselves—to strive for something that transcends what they are experiencing now. This is why all of the great prophets said, "What you seek you will surely miss." The most dedicated efforts of years of seeking can only lead to one place—and that is to creatively express oneself in the "Now" moment only.

Ironically, the simplest of souls are more in touch with the "Now" than those of us who are weighted down by too much education and too many plans.

A farm woman from the midwest was interviewed on a television quiz show. After being asked where she lived, the moderator queried, "Have you lived there all your life?" The woman, who was well on in her years brusquely answered, "Not yet." Truly, she was in complete touch with the "Now" of her Sun. The more one is able to relate to this concept the easier one's life becomes. Karma, which is so much the result of past actions, exists only in very small measure in the "Now." The greatest "Karma" that exists in the "Now" is based upon the willingness to express one's solar energy in a creative and productive manner. By doing this, the drudgery, weights and burdens of life, disappear. The individual who is after all, only an actor, is able to play his role perfectly. He is the star of his universe.

One of the reasons why most people find it extremely difficult to stay in the "Now" of their Sun is because there is temptation everywhere not to do so. But here, again, the seeds of admiration, jealousy and the desire for pride over others, the very ancient principles that the Bible itself spoke about, along with man's inability to live up to them, all keep people from realizing the full power of their own Sun sign. By living the "Now" only, man soon discovers that he has more energy than he knows what to do with. His negative attitudes become virtually non-existant. And in those moments when he does experience friction, it passes quickly, for he doesn't allow his being to dwell in that which no longer is. But it takes a powerful boldness to live in the sunshine of the "Now," because this means that man does not have the handles of his future or his past to hold onto. There is a famous Zen story entitled "The Muddy Road," which aptly describes this point. Two monks were crossing a muddy road whereupon they encountered a young lady who was hesitant at crossing the road for fear of soiling her clothing. One of the monks picked her up and carried her across the muddy road. The other monk was silent. Later that evening as the two dined together, the monk who had been silent could no longer hold his feelings in. He chastized his friend saying, "You know that monks are not supposed to carry pretty young girls." The other monk was silent for a moment and then looking at his friend, replied, "I put her down at the edge of the road. Why are you still carrying her?" Here we see a perfect example of two friends trained in the same doctrine, dedicated to the same purpose in life, but each living a different "Now." The monk who carried her across the road and then put her down, made no more of the incident than what it actually was. During the rest of the walk, he enjoyed the scenery, the sunshine of the day. And, later that evening enjoyed his dinner, was satisfied with his answer to his friend who chastized him, and in all ways displayed the fact that he was capable of experiencing the "Now." The second monk may forever live, befuddled by doctrines, theories, roles, and measuring himself against another. Through all his studies he does not display the "Now."

We and our companions and travelers through life are born with different Sun signs which allow us to experience the "Now" in different ways. It is clearly not the different experiences of the different Sun signs that shape our lives so much as our ability to learn how best we can use our Sun sign to be in the "Now." External conditions are always changing. Moments move into other moments, but the "Now" does not change, for it transcends tomorrow and yesterday and after and before. The "Now" of your Sun sign is here right now! It is not, as Jesus said, "The Kingdom of Heaven is near at hand"—it is in fact "at hand" all the time.

Robert Browning said, "A man's reach should always exceed his grasp." This is the point of view of so many who miss the "Now" through being over anxious to experience what they will be in the future. The amazing thing is that no matter how much a man tries to be in his past or in his future, the "Now" keeps impressing itself upon him until he recognizes it. Thus, one has the choice of allowing external circumstances to force him to be in the "Now" or to radiate from the center of his being all of the creative power that the "Now" affords him.

Be your Sun, and your Sun sign. There is absolutely nothing wrong with it. In fact, there is no right or wrong in the "Now." Everything just is. And, by allowing yourself to just be, you will be able to discover the vast plentitude of all you are. If you do things for the approval of others, you will lose your solar spontaneity. Furthermore, you will find yourself growing more and more uncentered, as you yield to the past and future desires of those whose acceptance you think you need. The "Now" of the Sun can only be experienced by fully accepting yourself, and then using this acceptance to express, radiate, and experience all you have discovered.

To understand how to use your Sun to stay in the "Now" requires much conscious effort. This is why Karma keeps repeating itself every moment that an individual lets go of his awareness of his solar presence. Each moment that he grows more in touch with the power of being that his Sun affords him, repetition of past Karma dissipates more and more, for his focus of energy grows closer and closer to the only reality there is—the "Now."

## THE MOON AND THE NOW

The Moon has no light of its own. It only reflects the light of the Sun. As such it is a mirror of the solar self. In essence it is a reflection of reality.

Through the Moon an individual seeks to understand his alter ego. He tries to view the impressions others have of him, but every time he does this, he leaves himself. Looking at himself through other's eyes, he grows more and more confused as to who he really is, for the mirror is constantly changing.

The Moon holds rulership over one's memory. Here is where man can easily trick himself, for Karma is based very much on memory. What one truly does not remember (even unconsciously) does not exist in the "Now." But, the constant repetition of phobias, traumas, and past experiences keep bringing the past into the "Now," which conversely brings the "Now" back into the past. If one is not aware of how this works, it becomes very easy to experience a kind of sliding "Now" through one's Moon sign. This sliding "Now" can greatly diminish the power of the Sun. One cannot walk in different directions at the same time with the expectation of going anywhere, arriving anywhere, or, in fact, being anywhere at all. Most people vividly remember incidents that occurred twenty to forty years ago much better than they do thoughts and feelings that they experienced ten seconds ago. Gurdjieff, one of the great mystical teachers, constantly stressed the concept of what he called "Self-Remembering." How many times do we see a person walk across a room, get half-way to their destination and forget the reason why they walked in that direction in the first place. This type of individual is not practicing "Self-remembering." Instead, he is using his Moon to wander through that which no longer exists, clouding the present. The proper use of one's Moon is to be able to view the self as it is happening. Thus, one is able to be one's actor (through the Sun) and one's audience, producer, director and critic (through the Moon) all at the same time.

One should not try to memorize that which can be easily looked up in an available book. There is a limit to how much one can store in one's memory, and the more one tries to clutter this "storehouse" the more cloudy the Moon's mirror becomes. Remember your actions as you are doing them. This is the key to being in the "Now." When they are done, forget them, or you will lose the

"Now." Most people experience a great deal of lunar lingering as they are constantly sifting through memories which have little to do with the present moment. This creates habits that are often very difficult to break. There are no "habits" in the "Now," instead there is a fresh birth of experience, through which a feeling of newness exists everywhere.

In order for man to be himself through his Sun, he must be able to see himself through his Moon. But, he must not confuse *seeing* with *being*. Too many individuals try to be their Moon, or the reflection of themself rather than their true self. This is easy to slip into because in our environment, it seems natural to try to please others. Thus, we use our Moon to display emotions which we feel are expected of us. We smile when we want to retain a friendship. We scream when we want to end one. Later, we sift through our lunar reactions to see if they were appropriate, never fully realizing that they were only a reflection of how we try to see ourself through the eyes of others.

The Moon allows us to feel the "Now." It puts us in touch with our physical body, which is not the same as it was yesterday nor the way it may be tomorrow. It gives us a receptivity to the changing world around us and prompts us to grow. We are, certainly, to remember the past (on unconscious levels in order to feel a foundation to our being) but we are always to realize instantaneously that it is not occurring "Now." The trap that most of us fall into is that the moment past memories rise to conscious awareness (which the desire for evolvement seems to prompt) we tend to believe we are reliving it. This brings the past into the "Now" with such vividness that it actually replaces the "Now" and we lose contact with the correct priority of time. Long-standing patterns of reacting are deeply rooted in the Moon. An individual reacts to a situation in much the same way as he has always reacted to similar situations in the past. By doing this, he never fully realizes that the present situation is all that exists in the "Now," whose only relation to the past is often what he makes it. Astrology does not like to believe in the word "coincidence." The very thought of it puts a flaw in the perfect puzzle that Astrology is trying to solve. Everything in the universe is ordered according to one cosmic law or another. But in order to understand reality, one must first confront the fact that one of the cosmic laws is the Law of Disorder. Wherever something exists, something also does not exist. Wherever there is perfection, there is imperfection. Wherever there is order, there is disorder. And wherever there is a perfect puzzle, there is coincidence! This is the true reality of the universe we live in. For every way in which Astrology works, it does not work. And that is what makes it so intriguing. For every Moon sign that has a specific meaning, there are at least a thousand other meanings. How, then, is an individual to develop his belief system in anything at all, if belief itself (which is so much influenced by the Moon) is and is not two sides of the same reality? What a man believes to be true, based upon his feelings, becomes true for him. It is a believable truth that you are reading this sentence right now. But a moment from now that will not be the truth. Thus, an individual's belief system, based upon how he uses his Moon, should be fluid and changing with the ever-present "Now" rather than fixed or attached to past memories and then trying to conveniently fit the present into what was once comfortable.

A man's reflection of himself, as seen through his Moon, is forever changing. One day he looks in the mirror and likes himself. An hour later he looks in the mirror and doesn't. Then he fights himself to try to return to the ways he saw himself when he liked himself. The Moon rules growing, but are we to cut branches off a tree so that it will always retain its appearance when we last liked it, or are we to allow that tree to grow, and blossom, and fulfill itself to its ultimate potential?

The more man looks at himself through his moon, the more he will realize these constant changes. They are not from hour to hour or day to day, but actually moment to moment and each moment is a "Now" that is very real; not to be thrown into the context of what man thought he was in the past but to be experienced in the full, vivid richness of the present.

Man moves through time or gets stuck in time according to his own choosing. He can emotionally jam his present by past burdens that no longer exist or he can allow himself to flow with the current of his ever-changing present. The moon gives him this choice. Naturally, it is easier to constantly relive one's past because in each new situation the individual will continue to react in ways which are familiar to himself. Thus, he feels somewhat centered; or perhaps, to be more accurate, more familiar with the self he knows. But this very desire to be familiar with oneself keeps a person from the realization of the cosmic self that is not only forever changing but is at every moment a part of everything. This is the true feeling of the "Now." It is one of the most unbelievable things a person can realize; for the moment he does, he becomes stripped of his lunar womb and born into a new reality. No longer is he merely an observer to the world around him. Instead, he is the world around him. He begins to realize how much he hurts when he hurts another person. He begins to feel the pain, the suffering, the sorrow, the misery, the despair, and the joy, the happiness, the excitement, and the beauty of all that is around him. He knows the feel of weather conditions and his body bends and flows with such changes, much the same as the trees, the flowers, and all the rest of nature, of which he has become a part.

The Moon teaches us that no man is an island but that every emotion felt is part of a cosmic stream in which the individual self is floating. Sometimes there are ripples in the water, or high waves. And, other times the waters are calm and clear. The stream of emotions, however, is never the creation of one man alone. The belief that we have control over our emotional lives is a complete fallacy and it is from this fallacy that most of man's unhappiness stems for he is trying constantly to get a grip on himself. He seeks to establish a stream of emotions within himself that he can count on, at will, to work for him in order to achieve his desired ends. But ends are based on means and means of a stream come from the mutual creation of every drop of water within it. The moment man realizes this, he gives up the emotional battles within himself in order to win the war. As he looks at himself, he comes to realize that not all is his fault and not all isn't. He stops trying to defend against others who effect his emotions, for the more he tries to do this, the more he stays angry at his past and loses his "Now." Instead, he confronts the reality that others can have an effect on his emotions rather strongly, but by also looking at the converse of this he can discover how much he effects the emotions of others. Thus, instead of spending his emotional life trying to sort out who is impinging on whom, he learns how to accept himself and others as part of a cosmic flow that is forever changing in the "Now."

The man who does not remember yesterday is truly blessed for he is gifted with the ability to experience his full gamut of emotions today. He will not see one reflection of himself, he will see many. And, none is more true or false than another. He is able to stop emotional competition with others, replacing it with the acceptance of how easy it is for him to blend with all he is exposed to. He learns that some reflections of himself feel more desirable than others, but he never forgets that these are only reflections, sometimes clear, sometimes distorted, sometimes vague or abstract, and sometimes right to the point. Nevertheless, through all of these changing reflections which allow him to experience the full richness of the "Now", he must come to understand that the him that is his true reality is his Sun, not his Moon.

Most people try to spend their entire lives attempting to find a sameness between their Sun and their Moon. Even in horoscopes where the Sun and the Moon appear in the same zodiac sign the desire to identify one with the other can take a person away from his "Now" experience. The Sun completes its cycle once each year. The Moon, in turn, takes only twenty eight days. In a single day, the Sun stays at approximately the same degree. Meanwhile, the Moon moves approximately twelve degrees. If the "Now," for any given person, may be thought of as one day, look at the difference between the solar "Now" and the lunar "Now". There is a sameness to the Sun quality while the Moon moves through at least twelve different degrees of emotional experience in a single day. Twelve is a very mystical number, symbolizing fulfillment and completion. And here man must come to realize that fulfillment and completion are not necessarily based on the retaining of sameness, but instead, on experiencing the cosmic flow of change that makes a man see himself as twelve different men in a single day. He is good, he is evil, he is stingy, he is generous, he is loving, he is hateful, he is blessed and he is cursed, he is damned and he is redeemed. He is all of these things in a single day. In the cosmic here and "Now" which you are passing through from word to word in this sentence, he is all of these things in a single moment.

It is the acceptance of this true reflection of man, through his lunar mirror, that can bring him to emotional Karmic harmony with himself and his universe.

A great teacher once said, "All men are mad," for the changeability of their emotional nature shows that they truly stand for nothing. This is the emotional part of man, sometimes instinctual and oftentimes a mirror of his external environment. It is the way he flows through the stream of his "Now" consciousness. But always, it is important to remember, that while everything changes (through one's Moon sign) nothing changes in the "Now" of one's Eternal Self.

Knowing others is wisdom. Knowing the self is true enlightenment. Most individuals use their Moon sign to be receptive to feelings they get as a result of feedback through others. They try to see themselves emotionally through other people's eyes, hoping that each new person will reveal another facet of the self they cannot see. In effect, what they are doing, is asking other individuals to introduce them to themselves so that the ultimate goal of self-acceptance can one day be reached. This is very much how the mechanism of "meeting self" works but it should be understood that while one is going through the process of meeting oneself, one is not *being* oneself. Instead, the individual is divided between who he is and who he appears to be in the eyes of others.

The Moon has much to do with public image and whether one is famous, having a public of millions or thousands, or what one might consider more average, having a smaller public, consisting of friends, relatives and acquaintances, the concern over one's reflective image is nevertheless a departure from a oneness in being.

This oneness in being is achieved when the emotions (ruled by the Moon) arise from the self, rather than the external circumstances, people, and environment that the self observes. To look at one's self through another's eyes is to color one's view by their perception. Whatever psychological and emotional imperfections the other individual has (and they wouldn't be human if they didn't) will always shade and distort the way the individual sees himself. The moment one realizes that these outer perceptions of himself, in the ever-changing world around him, are not truly his here and "Now," he can become more in tune with his true nature. A leaf on a tree is exposed to the weather conditions but the ever-changing weather conditions are not the leaf. If the leaf forgets itself and becomes the weather conditions, it can no longer be the leaf. Thus, "remembering self" as stressed so much by Gurdjieff, Ouspensky and others is the principle key to the

"Now." Identifying with one's Sun rather than one's Moon will keep an individual from losing self in the ever-changing environment he is exposed to. We are to experience our environment as well as our place in it. But we are wasting tons of emotional energy which could be used for expressing creativity by carrying one moment into the next. When this is done each succeeding moment becomes only an echo of time already passed. Thus, the fresh, vivid newness the "Now" is lost by emotionally relating each new moment into patterns of the past.

The initial reaction to living in the "Now" for most people is quite frightening. This is because the security banisters or anchors that one has placed in the past and in the future no longer exist. One starts to feel either aloneness or a separateness from one's former self. This is where the beauty of the "Now" begins. If programmed habits from the past no longer exist and the doubts one has about living up to one's expectations in the future do not have to be dealt with, then what is one to do with the great emptiness in this very special place where past and future meet and dissolve each other?

First, one experiences a dissolving of the ego. Past reasons for motivating the self no longer exist. The desire for future gain from achievement or accomplishment is also non-existant. Thus, what is an individual to do with himself? At first he feels like he is in a state of limbo. Not being in the places and times that he has been accustomed to, he must look at himself through his Moon on more realistic levels. His work, whatever it may be, can no longer be for the purpose of pleasing others. The way he spends his day can no longer be for the building of his tomorrow. An emotional numbness must be confronted as the "Now" is neither stimulated nor drained by the past or future. Thus, the individual must learn how to stimulate and motivate himself from within. He must learn how to unite with his own emotions; for only when this is done can he stop draining himself and become one with whatever he is being and feeling at the present moment. The emptiness or voidness that one first experiences when confronting the "Now", although it initially causes conflicts to surface along with the full gamut of emotional responses, is, amazingly enough, the one and only solution to these conflicts. As each conflict arises in the mind, it is solved almost at the speed of light, for to dwell on it or go back to it means losing the "Now." Conflict is not created within an individual unless the mind already knows the solution. Thus, to confront the "Now" means to accept the fact that many of man's conflicts are his way of avoiding the "Now" experience. When the Moon is used negatively an individual can spend his entire lifetime complaining about all the things he could be and could do but somehow never seems to. When the Moon is used positively, an individual's expression of self (his being) and his reflection occur in harmony with each other.

He soon discovers that he has a great deal of time on his hands, while simultaneously understanding that the entire world of experience is open to him. This, too, is frightening, for he hardly knows what to do with himself within the great expanse of what he has discovered. At first there is difficulty seeing the light, because once an individual has harmonized both luminaries he becomes his own light. From that point, it is up to him to radiate and reflect simultaneously from himself, through himself, for the expression of his being in the "Now."

# Chapter Five

# THE INNER PLANETS AND "THE NOW"

## *MERCURY AND THE NOW*

Mercury is the planet of presence. It symbolizes the energy of all thought arising in the conscious mind. In the course of a single day thousands of thoughts flow through one's consciousness. Mercury is the fine filter through which one is able to dismiss or accept those thoughts which can be acted on in the "Now."

When an individual is not using his Mercury properly he tends to dissipate himself in different directions that rob him of his sense of presence. There is a direct quality to Mercury that brings thought to the point so that an individual can express ideas to others and to himself with a crisp clarity of understanding. Mercury holds rulership over all that is mundane, the very things that spiritual aspirants try to avoid. But there is nothing more spiritual than being in touch with the mundane; doing, acting, thinking clearly at all times so that one's entire being never loses its focus in the "Now" experience. As the planet of communication, Mercury's greatest message is that once one speaks words, they are not his any more. He has taken thought from his "Now" and given it to another. If he tries to hold on to such thoughts after expressing them, he will automatically keep sinking into other people's consciousness. Thus, to express a thought or an idea and to follow that idea through the mind of another so that they understand it the way we want them to understand it, is the easiest and most subtle way of losing our own "Now." When we understand that once we have expressed a thought, it is no longer ours, then there is room for a new thought to arise in place of the original one we have given.

Because of its insistence on preciseness, accuracy, and definition, Mercury is the perfect balance for Neptune. If an individual is sitting in a fog or is depressed and does not have an awareness of what is causing it but instead, keeps sinking deeper in trying to find the causes, the perfect way back to reality is through his Mercury. He must force himself to get up and develop an interest in all of the mundane thoughts and activities that could fill his day. Amazingly enough, as soon as he does this the fog or depression seems to lift. Mercury is a planet of constant activity and it is through the focusing of one's activities that an individual is able to center himself in whatever he is and whatever he is doing in the here and "Now." Non-emotional in nature, Mercury does not allow the mind to wander. Instead, its constant thought stream perpetuates an individual to express his vivid presence each moment. You will notice the enormous sense of presence that Geminis and Virgos have (both ruled by Mercury) in their ability to consciously handle so many things at the same time. These two signs refuse to fall into "the mystical sleep"—that dream world stemming from whatever takes one away from the reality of his presence.

When sexual thoughts divert one from one's center, the asexual quality of Mercury can help an individual refocus himself so that his energies are mentally directed in his "Now" rather than dissipated through primal expectancy urges in the future or remembrances of a past that no longer exist.

Mercury is the planet of doing and no sooner is something done then it is done. The thought or deed is already in the past. Through this understanding of how to use Mercury, an individual learns how to function at optimum efficiency realizing capabilities that he never thought he had. In many places of business we have seen the sign, "If you have nothing to do, don't do it here." This is another way of saying that there is much to be done in the present moment—so much, in fact, that any lapse in concentration will lead an individual away from himself. Thoughts follow each other like sheep following the shepherd. The sheep are not conscious of why they are following the shepherd, but the shepherd is conscious of every sheep in his flock. Mercury is the shepherd of one's thoughts. It can calm the unconscious through reason and logic. It can soothe the emotions by leading them to the here and "Now." As ruler of the five senses, Mercury becomes of prime importance when we deal with the questions of perception. Whatever an individual perceives, he must somehow deal with. Whatever an individual does not perceive, he does not have to deal with. Thus if an individual makes up his conscious mind, ruled by Mercury, to live in the "Now" then his perception will grow more and more focused in the moment and, little by little, everything that is outside of his "Now" will begin to find it's proper distance outside of his conscious perception.

Many individuals believe that it is a spiritual goal to become conscious of everything. This is nonsense. Only God in His all knowing could be conscious of everything. Man's attempt at such folly can only lead him away from himself. Mercury is the planet of understanding. Some people are constantly trying to understand others and use their perceptions to focus on other people's lives. There is no question that a fine understanding of others is wisdom. But, as mentioned earlier, the fact remains that understanding the Self is enlightenment. And, there is a big difference between wisdom and enlightenment. Furthermore, the path leading towards wisdom is not the same as the path leading towards enlightenment. There have been very many wise-men in the history of the world, but there have been very few enlightened souls.

The personal enlightenment that Mercury can offer comes not from minding the business of others, but rather from focusing all of one's conscious attention on what is happening in one's own personal "Now" experience.

You cannot change the thoughts of others for they will resist you. But you certainly can be the shepherd of your own flock. Through it's child-like qualities, Mercury does not question the distant future nor regret the errors of the past. Even mental journeys are short and quick, never losing sight of where "home-base" is. Thus an individual can use his Mercury as a centering device for all levels of thought he experiences. When he finds himself going too deep into the mysteries of the universe and wondering if he will ever be able to find his way back he can use his Mercury to wash a dish, clean a room, water his plants, or look at greeting cards at the local stationery store. Mercury is the planet of being in contact with the sharp, crisp, vividness of the "Now" reality.

We all, from time to time, experience tendencies to daydream and drift to places and times that are not part of the "Now." The more we do this, the more we grow discontented with whatever we are experiencing "Now." Thus we begin to believe in the greener pastures of other people's lives. This kind of drifting is the beginning of negative thinking and negative thinking is the beginning of negative Karma. One must become conscious of one's thinking in order to see how easily it can keep one centered or lead one away from one's path.

As the planet of mundane communication, consider the workings of Mercury in the following example. An individual rings your doorbell and says, "Hi, how are you?" You smile and answer, "Fine, how are you?" Ninety-nine percent of the time the next question arising from your friend will be, "HOW HAVE YOU BEEN?" The moment you consider this question worthy of an answer you have lost the "Now." But, by your staying in the reality of your "Now" the individual you are speaking to is forever answering every question he asks.

When Mercury is used in this manner its most positive quality—efficiency—becomes quite apparent. The fact is that people really have very little of importance to say to each other. They constantly draw on their past and the unknown qualities of their future to define their "Now" experience. This happens because they lose the "Now" constantly by refusing to be the shepherd of their flock of conscious thoughts. The most fascinating thing about understanding the scope of the "Now" through one's Mercury is that as large as it is, it is small enough for an individual to truly focus himself in time and space. Once he learns how to lead his own thought streams, paying avid attention to every sheep in his flock, he is able to see clearly how the use of language causes Karmic manipulations.

One of the biggest problems most individuals have, in terms of establishing their own inner peace and tranquility comes from the misuse of the combined function of the Moon and Mercury. Through memory and habit patterns, established in the past (the Moon), they have set up within themselves a type of emotional-mental digiting process. This process works in the following way: when an individual is confronted with any external stimuli, he feeds it through his mental-emotional computer, and because he is programmed the way he has always been programmed, the little digits in that computer (Mercury) or his own particular mathematical sequence of thought processes always bring about the same reaction to stimuli. Thus, as long as an individual uses this type of mental-emotional digiting process in his everyday life he will continue to react to each new stimulus in the same ways he has always reacted to them in the past. What is he doing? He is taking the "Now" and making it fit his past expectations. He is using an old computer trying to solve new problems that it has not yet been programmed for. He is, in fact, taking the "Now" and distorting it through whatever experiences he has had in the past. It is from this type of mental-emotional reaction patterns that man not only loses the "Now" but also deludes himself into thinking and believing that he has controlled his past and can continue to do so in the present. Most of all these patterns leave him literally a nervous wreck in terms of dealing with his environmental circumstances.

The minute an individual is able to see his own digiting process and to control it his entire nervous system begins to calm down. At the same time, his mental processes are free to focus on finer things.

Mercury is the planet of relationships. In this sense, it not only rules relationships between people and things but it rules causal relationships and spatial relationships. When cause and effect are seen clearly through Mercury in the "Now," the individual is able to develop an accurate sense of perspective through which cause and effect, time and space are clearly defined. Clarity of perception is one of the greatest gifts man has for without it he cannot define himself or his relationship with the universe in which he lives. Thus, it becomes important for a person to learn that Mercury, which rules his intellect, his perceptions, his digital reactions, and his general state of mind, creates and solves Karma through every word he speaks and every thought he has as well as those he listens to.

It is through Mercury that one is able to accept the smallness of oneself in comparison to the vastness of a universe that one knows so little about. The *Tao Te Ching* states, "He who stands on tiptoes is not steady." The principle function of Mercury is not to project thoughts into the future or to other places nor to computerize one's perceptions in order to create judgmental opinions or bigoted attitudes. When used properly, Mercury allows one simply to function in the here and "Now." Mankind always tends to make the simple very complex and is then confronted with the problem of bringing the complex back to the simple. In its childlike simplicity Mercury is at its best use when an individual is doing all he can to function to the best of his ability right "Now." But, here one should be aware that Mercurial thought occurs so fast that one can trick oneself into not seeing the "Now" by trying to link up what you are reading "Now" with what you may have read several pages earlier. The constant mind game is "But how will I remember?" By trying to remember the past in order to widen the present you are missing the point of what is happening right "Now." In fact, it would lead you to thoughts like, "And I always used to think. . . " "Now" see where that leads! Notice how far removed from the "Now" you have become in only a fraction of a second.

Interest in the "Now" is one of Mercury's finest qualities. It keeps an individual in tune with an everhappening present. And, remember it is the ruler of Gemini and Virgo, both mutable signs. This is further indication of the fact that the "Now" is presently changing. Thus, one's greatest method of being in the "Now" is to understand that one is constantly changing with it. This does not mean that one should be overly sensitive to the changes in one's external environment, for it is the "Now" within the Self that is constantly changing. And when you really get down to it, what can be more important than an individual's acceptance of his relationship with himself within his everchanging "Now?"

## VENUS AND THE NOW

As the planet of love and harmony, Venus works best for the individual who is able to see beauty in all things. When one can do this, there is no need to let the Self dwell in great loves from the past, or beautiful moments long gone by. Because, in essence, the full wealth of beauty is in the "Now." Venus is the planet of contentment and gratitude. In its utter simplicity, it rules the balance of nature. In the course of a single day it is almost impossible not to pass a tree, a patch of grass, a living plant, a painted picture, or hear music, or a poem or see a smile. There is beauty all around if we just open our eyes and our senses to it. There is beauty in machines, sidewalks, pavements, automobiles, etc. There is a living kaleidoscope of color that exists in every moment. Our senses, our bodies, and our minds cannot resist absorbing it constantly.

At the same time there is great beauty, harmony, and love within each of us, if we would only allow it to surface. The soft, gentle vibration of Venus is very much a part of the "Now" experience. Consider an individual going into a department store to buy some shirts. He walks over to the counter, finds the selection of shirts that are his size, quickly picks up three in different color assortments, pays for them at the register, and leaves the store. He has performed a chore that he knew was necessary. In the future, he will wear these shirts at different times in accordance with the same attitude he had when he bought them. They are a necessity and he will think no more of it.

This type of individual is not at all in touch with the Venus vibration in the "Now." If he were, he would have walked over to the shirt counter, picked up a shirt that pleased him, held it in his hands, and then asked himself the question, "Do I really love this shirt?" "Do I really love the way this shirt feels around my body as much as I love the arms of a woman I love doing the same thing?" "Does the shirt make me love myself?" "Does the shirt love me?" By experiencing all of these feelings and making the decision to buy the shirt based on such feelings, not only is the person experiencing the full richness of the "Now" in the present, but imagine what his future "Nows" will be like every time he wears that shirt. Thus, how he reacts right now in such a simple matter as buying a shirt, creates both present and future Karma. But let us not even think of the future, for it is not here yet. Let us consider the joy of the "Now." The simple purchasing of anything which we go through every day, is either a chore or a great act of love. The air itself literally breathes love every moment. It fills the lungs and the body with the fine soft essence of harmony. There is a flowing gentleness within one's being that softens the thought patterns and calms the turbulence of the unconscious, if one is willing to allow oneself to experience the fine harmony of Venus. When you look at a simple greeting card, don't just look at it—for then the mind is somehow silently telling you that it is just a greeting card; not too different from millions of others that you have seen in the past. Instead, feel the texture of the paper. When you do this, it becomes the only greeting card in your "Now." Look at the colors on the card—the beauty of the artwork, and the poetry, and let it bring a smile to your face as you and the card are all that exists in experiencing the vibration of the Venus in the "Now." Once you have made the decision to buy the card, do not dwell in it; for the "Now" has already passed. And, there is much more beauty, harmony, and happiness that you

can easily miss by living in a moment, however beautiful it
was, that no longer is!

Walk around your room, and look at the objects in
it. See them as if you are perceiving them for the first time.
These are the things you love. And, you love them deeply.
If there are objects in your room that you do not feel this
way about, throw them away right *now,* for every time you
perceive them you are perceiving something less than love.
Since there is a powerful tendency for us to momentarily
identify with our perceptions, why should not every object
you own be what you love the most. Venus rules
possessions. By loving what you have at every moment a
great peace begins to develop within you, as you are
creating a Karma of contentment. However, this Karma of
contentment is not what one is working towards in the
future. For again, we can not pretend to know the future.
Instead, the contentment is "Now."

Do what you love, do not do what you don't love.
That way you stay in harmony with yourself.

In the Desiderata Prayer there is a line that says,
"never feign affection." There is a powerful reason for
this. All of us, in one way or another, have experienced
many hurts in the past. We are advised of the fact that time
heals all wounds. This is the furthest thing from the truth,
for the world is filled with millions of people hurt many,
many years ago and whether they like to show it or not, are
hurting still! The true healer of all wounds is love in the
"Now" where there is no time. When one is experiencing
love, hurts in the past miraculously disappear. But,it must
be love in the "Now" for the moment an individual tries to
protect the future security of love he is experiencing, he is
automatically unconsciously relating it to his past
insecurities. Love is. Love is "Now." Love is here. Accept
it!

When Jesus came to Earth and said, "The
Kingdom of Heaven is near at hand," he chose his words

very skillfully. On one level he meant that the Kingdom was there then and for those who would touch his hand the Kingdom would instantly become their "Now." But, he did not want to threaten those who feared and doubted, and the cynical ones who would destroy all that was good. Thus, by using the word "near" instead of "here" he allowed those who could know to know, while those who could not know would keep going through their mind digits thinking "How near is near? When, where, etc.?" Until enough accumulated thoughts and feelings would turn them away from Jesus, allowing him to do his work in the "Now." To this very day there is a living God in all things. But, only those who love know it. Have you ever noticed when people are in love, their hair shines, their eyes glisten, their cheeks are filled with color, and their bodies are robust with strength and vitality? But love is not only the love of another person. It is a love of life in all its forms. It is the ability to see beauty and meaning in everything.

Most of us seek love outside of the "Now" and therefore can never see it when we have it. We think that we might experience love in the future but we do not know how to be in touch with it at every moment. If you have a set of glasses with designs on them, pick one up right now and look at it. Some artist whom you never met drew that picture and gave it to you. All of its meaning, colors, and feeling are yours right "Now." How many times, in the course of a day, have you actually listened to the calling of birds? The pillow that you sleep on every night, that softens all of your thoughts and soothes you—is it just a pillow or is it something very special to you? If you smoke a cigarette or take a drink, are you doing it out of habit, out of nervousness, or because right "Now" it is truly what you love to do? The more you begin asking yourself these kind of questions, the more you will realize how easy it is to be out of touch with love in the "Now."

What have you done today to be in love with yourself? Even the most mundane chores should be like play in order to experience the love vibration. Most people have a tendency to make the false assumption that they are more delicate, sensitive, and tender inside, than others. Thus, others can hurt them. But, they never stop to consider the converse. Do others not have a gentleness, a tenderness, a softness, inside of them that makes them afraid of you? In order to experience love in the "Now" an individual must literally break down his false barriers, for Venus is not a planet of walls. Instead, it is a state of being, a way of seeing that life is love. The aesthetics of the "Now" are one's personal pleasure in being. When one is able to feel enough Venus in him as well as around him, both past and future disappear. But, the amount of Venus that an individual is able to see in his external environment depends entirely upon how much love he is willing to let himself feel inside. When a person is punishing himself for past reasons, whatever they may be, he cannot feel his Venus for he willfully separates himself from all the good that is presently inside him.

In the same way that there is a digiting function between the Moon and Mercury which tends to preprogram a person's opinion, there is also a similar function in the combination of Mercury and Venus. A person starts to experience love through his Venus and then his Mercury says, "But." He tries again, and again his Mercury says, "But." This continual process impedes the natural flow of Venus. While one might argue that it keeps a person from over-indulgence, it usually has the opposite effect. The individual finds a thousand reasons why he cannot experience the full richness of love that life offers him. Again, the digiting process is based on the past and once a person realizes this, the natural outpouring of Venus without the "Buts" in-between can happen.

Although astrology sees many similarities between the Moon and Venus, there is one very big difference between the two. The Moon has much to do with self-remembering but Venus has to do with the actual *feeling* of the Self. While there seems to be a fine line between the two this is not really the case. The Moon is a reflection of one's self-acceptance. Venus is the true acceptance! As the ruler of Libra and Taurus, the rays of Venus represent balance and centering as well as contact with earthly reality. There is physical beauty and there is ethereal beauty and there is a blend between the two. When man is in contact with this blend, he is able to experience fulfillment on different levels. However, it is only through an awareness of these levels within the Self that an individual is able to sense, even in the slightest way, all the beauty around him.

Interestingly enough, when a person experiences a great deal of love, beauty, and harmony in the "Now" he tends to stay in the present. Conversely, when love and beauty seem to be absent from his life he tends to drift into his past, seeking in memories to restore that which he truly would like to feel "Now." This is a natural human reaction, but with a little effort an individual can find enough beauty in the "Now" so that it magnetizes his present more than his past. It should be understood that this takes effort to achieve. Venus is also the planet of possessions. Personal love can often get possessive and personal loves from the past carry with them a possessive magnetism that keeps luring a person back to that which no longer exists in his reality. Thus, the effort necessary to stay in the "Now" involves filling your life with enough Venus so that there is no room or reason for the past to seep into the present.

Since the "Now" is also so much a product of the here, it becomes important for a person to realize how they have formed love attachments to places which brought them past happiness. Although places seem very different from each other they are in many ways symbolically alike. Any traveler will tell you that there is practically no town in the United States that doesn't have its own Main Street. There is no country road that doesn't have trees, very similar to trees in other places. There are many streets that one can drive down, which might well be called, "Anywhere U.S.A." It is through the observation of simple scenic beauty, which we all do so much of the time, that we tend to compare and remember the beauty of other places we have been in the past. The thought or the feeling may only last a fraction of a second. In fact, it usually occurs so fast that it is barely noticeable, unless one is truly aware. But the important point is this: when the aesthetics of a present scene are similar to a scene from the past, there is a strong tendency for the gentle, lulling qualities of Venus to momentarily daze the clarity of our vision. By the slightest comparison of a present scene with a past one, an individual brings back to mind the collective incidents, events, and people associated with the aesthetic nature of the scene he is re-experiencing. Whenever this occurs he loses the "Now" and his reactions to the world of beauty in the "Now" are less a product of the present then somewhere in the past. It is because of Venus's gentle persuasion that this is so difficult to notice. A kind of relaxed laziness (one of the more notable negative qualities of Venus) tends to set in by allowing one subtle feeling after another, perhaps thousands of them in a single minute, to accumulate to the point where they tend to pervade the entire being. The individual believes he is experiencing calmness, but in truth, he is re-experiencing his past. His vibration becomes lowered and by doing this hour after hour or day after day, he soon becomes a product of lethargic complacency. He loses his desire to function in the "now" because he has covered it with so much of the past that he cannot see it.

The Venus experience in the "Now" can be extremely beautiful, loving, and harmonious without lowering one's vibration rate. Again, this takes the willingness to make an effort to see beauty in all things, all people, and most of all, yourself right now, right here.

Venus has much to do with nature. Consider the beauty of a plant. It's bottom leaves constantly fall away as new ones grow on top. The bottom leaves were new in the past, but they are not beautiful to the plant "Now." In the same way, nostalgic thoughts of past loves are like a person dwelling on his bottom leaves, which have already dropped off and been replaced many times.

As the ruler of Libra, Venus can sometimes have a rather obstinate quality, feeling both sides of things, but often missing the center. As the ruler of Taurus, it can have a stubborn quality, which persistently holds on to past values, not allowing the "Now" to happen. Instead of being the victim of these two negative characteristics of Venus, one can experience the "Now" best by vibrating to this planet's finest quality and that is to become part of it's fullness and richness in all things, in all people, in all that is around you, and all that is within you, right "Now"—right here! Look at how full your present is "Now" and allow a rich sense of contentment and gratitude to permeate your entire state of being. This is the "Now" of Venus and it is very real.

## MARS AND THE NOW

Mars is the planet of desire and movement. It is constantly stimulating the "Now" and filling it with a vivid sharpness that keeps re-awakening one's consciousness. The most common misuse of the Mars energy is to project one's desires so far into the future that it makes one's actions in the "Now" seem meaningless. This causes discontent, unrest, and a constant state of frustration. The Mars of the "Now" is based on spontaneity. Mars adds movement to what otherwise might seem a reality of no progress. It should not keep projecting the individual beyond whatever he is doing in the present, but rather, it should stimulate his present with the vitality he needs in order to experience it. If a person keeps projecting his hopes and desires long into the future or would like to re-enact that which he has already been through then he is constantly losing vitality. He experiences an energy drain and may think it is coming from other people, when it is his own inability to act in his "Now."

Mars is the planet of motivation. It is the mover of ideas into action. If one carefully observes the stimulation of Mars something very interesting reveals itself. Motivation to act comes quickly, perhaps many times in a single moment. But, it also passes just as quickly. Thus, if a person spends his life analyzing his motivations he tends to lose so many of them that, in essence, he loses motivation to do anything at all. The need to do comes quickly. In order to experience the "Now" one must follow one's needs and then, by letting them pass, new ones will arise in their place. In some ways, similar to the function of Mercury, the activity of Mars keeps one's vibration high and it is this rapid movement of one's vibration that leaves no room for depression, regret, or remorse.

Sometimes, Mars is primitive in its urges and does need some control through the wisdom of Saturn and the reason of Mercury, but never to the point where one inhibits, represses, and sublimates the powerful motivating energy that is stimulating him in the "Now." On it's raw level Mars does not question or analyze—it acts. And, it is through acting that man achieves a state of being. Every moment he is *becoming*. The joy of Mars is never in the reaching of one's ultimate goals, for when an individual reaches them, he may have long since forgotten the reason why he wanted them. Instead, the joy of Mars is to be found in one's constant state of becoming. This is the true source of motivation. Whatever one may ultimately achieve is far less important that his union with the act of becoming, which is the stimulating, moving, vibrant quality of his "Now" experience.

Man is a funny animal. He tends to be at his happiest when he knows what he wants. When he ultimately achieves his wants and desires, he loses something. He must then decide what he really wants. If you walk up to different people and ask the question, "If you could have anything in the world, what is it that you want?" You would be amazed to find how difficult it is for people to answer you. The fact is, that it is not what man specifically wants that brings him happiness, instead, it is his acceptance of his desire nature in the "Now." Always, he will desire something and from time to time the desires will change. What is important is that desire itself is what motivates him at every moment. And, the less his desires are fulfilled the more he is motivated.

The Bible itself does not speak against desire—only against the misuse of it. What is important here is that an individual's desires are truly his own, rather than a carbon copy of what he sees around him. If he works a lifetime trying to achieve the desires of others, he will have lived a lifetime of other people's lives. In every moment he will not be in his own here or "Now." Instead, he will be tuned in to the desire nature of mass consciousness. This can only confuse his present moment, diffuse the vitality of his own space, and lead him into future times and places that have little to do with the reality of his "Now" experience.

The motivation for sexuality and creativity comes and is gone in the blinking of an eye but when either one is present, that is what is happening now. And, when neither is present, something else is happening in the "Now." It is not desire itself that can destroy a person, but rather the attachment to desire which keeps one lingering in desires that have already passed along with needs that have already been fulfilled.

If one were to sit down and truly confront his desire nature in a realistic way he would soon understand how erratic he truly is. In the course of a single day, a thousand desires having little to do with each other arise in the mind and in the body. Certainly one cannot act on all of these— nor should one go to the opposite extreme of self-denial; for neither will allow the individual to experience the energy level at which he is most comfortable. The focusing of energy is forever changing and the individual who is constantly trying to put his energy in one direction because he believes it will lead him to some future desired goal, may or may not achieve the goal. But, if he flows with the rise and fall of his energy pattern, he is achieving goals every moment. He may or may not achieve his lifetime goals but that is not the question here, because the goals of a lifetime take a lifetime to reach. Whether one desires to be conscious of them at every moment, or chooses to be more in touch with one's desire nature in the present, makes a very big difference as to how well a person is able to function right Now! Mars can make one the actor in his life, or the reactor to the lives of others. Regardless of what House it is placed in within the horoscope, Mars gives the individual the freedom to use his energies as he sees fit. Interestingly enough, whenever an individual refuses to use his own Mars by impressing his presence in whatever he is doing, he will find that others use their Mars on him. Where then, is the correct balance in how to use one's energies? If one impresses his Mars on others, one is constantly creating Karmic conditions. At the same time, if one allows others to impress their Mars on him, he becomes the receiver of their Karmic output. Lao Tsu, the great sage, said, "A good walker leaves no footsteps." In this very simple sentence he was alluding to the possibility of acting without Karmic repercussions. When the desire to act is not coupled with the desire to control the actions or reactions of others, then one is "walking without footsteps." At the same time, the desire to act should be blended with an understanding that one's actions are important enough to the self so that they need not be controlled by others. Thus, one becomes both the sower and the reaper of oneself. Within a world where so much seems the same, the individual can then establish his own unique identity. What greater gift could a man give himself, than himself?

How much does a person identify with what he does? How much is a man his deeds? And, conversely how much are his deeds a product of his own unique identity? Of all the planets in the zodiac, Mars is perhaps the most important and, at the same time, the most difficult one to deal with in terms of an individual finding out who he is! Whether he likes to recognize it or not, who he is at any given time depends very largely upon what he wants. If a man says, "I want to eat," then he is a hungry creature in that moment. After having eaten, the desire changes and with it, so does the man. The very nature of desire often makes man seem contradictory in his value systems. Sometimes he is in agreement with his desires and other times he is not. He desires to live now, but he also desires to preserve his future. At the same time he desires to hold on to his past. The simple fact is that man can only desire what he does not have. Thus, rather than spending one's energies on a future that is uncertain, a past that no longer exists, and a world of things that others have, man's only one real desire that can ever bring him happiness in the "Now" is the desire to be one with himself.

Ouspensky, in his book *In Search of the Miraculous,* says that there are different "I's" in one's being. Like separate personalities, each "I" thinks it is the ruler over the others—and for a moment, it is. But in the next moment, a different "I" will take over rulership and may or may not agree with the "I" that was ruling before. Each "I" in the personality structure has its own desires.

One "I" may impulsively desire to buy a $10,000 car. After agreeing to years of time payments, all the other "I's" must take on the responsibility and suffer the consequences of what the first "I" impulsively demanded. These other "I's" become angry at that "I" because they have desires of their own which are not being met. From this simple analogy one can see how confusing man's desire nature is. But, there is one way to eliminate these different desires stemming from the different "I's" in the personality. In order to do this, one must find the real "I",—the one whose desire nature is powerful enough to subjugate all the other "I's" because it is consistent with the soul's sincere desire to express itself through a harmonious personality.

Desire is not a bad thing. It is only when different desires fight each other that the "Now" becomes filled with inconsistencies, causing enough unhappiness in the individual for him to run to the future, the past or other places. Thus, the desire for oneness of mind is a good desire enabling the individual to focus his present actions to allow him to establish and retain oneness with himself.

Mars has two moons, Demos and Phoebos, which constantly orbit around the planet. It might well be possible that whichever moon is between Mars and the Earth at the time of birth has a great influence on how one relates to the Mars energy. It is entirely possible that when Demos is closer to the Earth, an individual tends to be demonstrative, outgoing, more impulsive, daring, courageous, and fully expressing outwardly the power of the Mars energy. Conversely, if the Moon Phoebos is closest to the Earth at the time of birth, more phoebic, inward, and repressed personalities are contained within the individual. This is only a theory, and future research will either prove or disprove its validity. But, it may well have much to do with the dominant "I" of one's desire nature. And, as these two Moons constantly orbit the planet, they may well be the explanation for the changing "I's" that constantly want to rule man's desire nature. Still, it should be remembered that any Moon is a reflection, a mirror, either a carbon copy or an inverted distortion of the original. Although desire is ever-changing in the ever-changing world one lives in, there is, on a much deeper level, desire that emanates from one's soul which is not only far more constant, but keeps an individual steady through the ever-changing circumstances to which he is subjected. Knowing this desire from one's soul is to know oneself.

More than any other planet, Mars is the key to one's self-identity. As ruler of Aries and the First House, as well as co-ruler of Scorpio and the Eighth House, Mars plays a big role in beginnings and endings—the conscious and the unconscious identity structure. When a man realizes that he is both the beginning and the end, but he is only one man (one entity unified with itself) during conscious and unconscious states of being, then he begins to function in the "Now." If he goes through life as the collective ID of everybody he has ever met, then there is no "Now" for him, for he is only a piecemeal collection of everybody else's lives. The moment he backs off from wanting to change others or desiring to better the world he lives in and confines himself to that one little corner of the universe which is his own unique psychic space, he will begin to confront the desire nature that emanates only from himself. As soon as he does this he progresses into his own "Now," understanding that it is the only reality in which he can truly function as himself.

Mars is the last of the inner personal planets. It is what a man desires to do with his life, his day, his hour, and his moment. But, even more than that, Mars represents what he is doing *right now* that will impress his own unique identity into the universal consciousness from the very small, but powerfully significant, role he plays in acting out the desire of his soul.

# Chapter Six

# THE OUTER PLANETS
# AND "THE NOW"

## *JUPITER AND THE NOW*

Jupiter is the first of the outer planets. We call it a co-consciousness planet because like all of the outer planets, it shares ideas and experiences which are more than personal. It symbolizes a cooperative, collective understanding, coming from what is available in the universal "Now" rather than what is more personal to the individual self. As the planet of expansion, it enlarges one's consciousness bringing an individual to the realization that he does not always see the Gestalt whole of his understanding. It loosens his hold on what he personally calls his own, freeing him to experience that which is larger than himself. He begins to understand that "Now" is happening on different levels at the same time.

Jupiter is the planet that rules places, and connects them with higher forms of thought. We have all at one time or another gone through experiences of being in one place but having momentary flashes (seemingly beyond our control) of other places. We know that, at the moment, we are not really in these other places but for a brief flash, we seem to be. If one observes these flashes, the reality of other places becomes as vivid and convincing, if not more so, than the physical reality of where one actually is at the moment.

Thus, in dealing with "The Now" which is also a function of "The Here," Jupiter brings one to the realization that in higher levels of thought, everywhere can be here, and here can be everywhere. We know that the mind can have a tendency to wander. Of all the signs in the zodiac, this occurs the most in Sagittarius where the effect of Jupiter is felt the strongest. Everything in "The Now" becomes expanded to the point that the individual seems to be confronted with literally millions of thoughts and ideas, many of which appear to have little to do with each other. Yet, they have much to do with each other, for they are all happening "Now." This is the reason why one's initial contact with Jupiterian energies tends to be a little confusing. The individual asks himself—what is going on?—as he begins to sense his own personal smallness within the scope of all he is starting to experience. He feels so many things, he hardly knows who he is. Decades, or centuries feel like only a moment. Entire books seem like only a single word. Thoughts no longer exist in a singular dimension. Instead, they become more like thought streams, running in many directions at the same time. When this is personalized, it tends to give the individual great impatience with himself. He constantly wants to follow each thought which, if he did, would undoubtedly lead him to experience everything his body, mind and soul could possibly handle. But again, it should be remembered that Jupiter is not one of the personal planets. Its effect on any one person is to bring about a higher awareness of the greater whole than the individual normally senses. He is part of that whole but he is not all of it, nor could he realistically ever hope to be.

    If you want to understand the effect of Jupiter, sit down and read a newspaper. But try your best to read each item at the same time. While you are doing this, put the radio on. But instead of one station, imagine yourself listening to all channels at the same time. Meanwhile, think of every piece of advice everyone has ever given you concerning all questions you have ever asked. But, don't stop here. Think of every place you have been and every place you may go to in the future. Think of every face you have ever known. Listen to every sound in the street that you can hear. One could continue this analogy endlessly but the point is that Jupiter is so much of what is happening *now* that it is unquestionably more than any one individual can sanely handle at a time. What Jupiter does is to make an individual aware of the whole world around him. However, if he is to retain any grip on himself at all, he must understand that from such a great wealth of opportunity, he must only draw on that which does not separate him from himself.

Jupiter is also the planet of higher language. Where Mercury holds rulership over words, Jupiter's effect is to make one aware of all the different languages being spoken through the same words. In this respect, the connotations of words, the double entendres, the thousands of suggestions that a single sentence may contain, become apparent. Sometimes, language itself seems like sheer stupidity. Jupiter is the proverbial tower of Babel. But, in silence, it is also the temple of Solomon's wisdom. Where Mercury influences the lower mind's personal thought processes, Jupiter rules the higher mind and all that it knows through impersonal thought processes. These thoughts are often difficult to verbalize, for not many individuals are in good contact with their higher mind. And, even those who are, usually only experience it in moments. Jupiter rules the law, the commandments of God, the understanding of a higher way of life. But it takes conscious effort on the part of any individual to learn how to get the most benefits from Jupiter while still staying focused in his personal experience. This is because Jupiter has a tendency to remove an individual so far from the "Mundane", that the ability to function on a day-to-day basis is lost because it seems so unimportant. Yet, the "Now" is today. Ask yourself, is Jupiter brightening your day, or removing you from it? The tendency to let one's mind wander to distant places and wider horizons is largely a product of how an individual can allow Jupiter to dissipate his "Now" into experiences that are beyond his true realty. On the other hand, when Jupiter is used with the understanding that "Here" is everywhere, then the individual is able to appreciate the fullness of all he is experiencing now without interrupting the continuity of his flow by too much future or distant expectation.

One of the most positive aspects of Jupiter's energy is its ability to loosen crystallized matter. It enables an individual to free himself from his past and rise above it by experiencing the richness of his present. Nature speaks to him from everywhere. And, he can begin to function in tune with the greater cosmic whole. Certainly, the energy of Jupiter symbolizes a loosening of Karmic weight. Instead of a constant refocusing of the mind on echoes of the past, the individual can become aware of everything that replaces it. At first the natural tnedency is to feel that the outer environment is distracting one from oneself. This is true but the harmonic beauty and truth that exists in the outer environment when it is blended with the higher inner being is also calling one away from the self-suffering and, in its place, gives an individual the enjoyment of experiencing clearly all that life has to offer him. The Now of Jupiter is achieved when one learns how to see the light instead of attempting to classify darkness.

## SATURN AND THE NOW

As the planet of responsibility, Saturn imposes its burdens on an individual so that he understands the importance of his own needs. By meeting his tasks to the best of his abilities, an individual gives form to his own self worth. This helps him to learn how to be contained as an individual. The interesting thing about Saturn is that while it has so often been thought of as the planet of restrictions, it is actually a planet of great freedom.* When one avoids the tasks and responsibilities that give meaning and purpose to one's existence, then there is no question that the weight of Saturn is felt heavily. All that an individual should confront but tries to ignore starts to gather weight in his mind. But, when a more positive approach is taken in dealing with the everyday obstacles which are only stepping stones towards one's evolution, the more one frees oneself from the weight of the past.

Saturn is the planet of Karma and makes an individual's life, in many ways, the result of his past actions. It crystallizes his past, like a wall which he must ultimately climb over in order to reach the present. The beauty of Saturn lies in the fact that it is also the planet of persistent effort and trying. It gives an individual the perseverance to climb that wall so that there is nothing between him and his present. No Astrologer in the world would be foolish enough to espouse the theory that past Karma is easily dissipated. Things take time. And, Saturn is the planet of time. The more an individual begins to understand the nature of Saturn, the more he is able to flow with time. Rather than brooding over past mistakes he learns how to spend each day crystallizing new form, new attitude, new purpose and new meaning to his life. The more he does this, the more the old drops away. Much like the torn and tattered pages of an old discarded book, Saturn's records of one's deeds and misdeeds ultimately give way to new purpose. Always, the new is an outgrowth of the old. It is up to the individual through his

---

* See *Saturn: Planet of Happiness,* Dell Horoscope Magazine, p. 39, August 1978, Dell Publishing Co., Inc., N.Y.

own wisdom and free will, coupled with the desire to use both, that past patterns which were self-defeating are not echoes in "The Now."

There is a tendency through Saturn for an individual to program his life. He spends years building ideas and giving form to all he thinks will make him happy. As a result, his computerized mind has a tendency to stereotype people and things in the world around him. He meets new people and new circumstances all the time, but tends always to compare them to the form he has set up in his mind. Not only is this unfair to the new people and the circumstance he meets, but it also keeps him building patterns which only keep rebuilding Saturn's wall.

In order to flow with the best energies of Saturn, an individual must be ready to truly confront himself. What he is building in the here and now must be a firm foundation beneath his feet. He must learn not to dissipate himself on thoughts or actions that are unproductive. By doing this, he starts to sense a youthfulness in the Now. The more he senses this, the less he needs to reach for the past and the future and, at the same time, the less he needs to reach for other places, beyond where he is at any given moment. The sense of containment that Saturn affords is not a restriction at all, but merely teaches an individual how to mold himself in the ways which have the most meaning. This sense of containment brings a certain silence with it. The individual learns that the more he talks about what he wants to do, the less purpose he feels in doing it. In silence he conserves his forces and is able to dedicate every moment towards achieving his purpose. This is not an easy thing to do; it takes concentrated effort. However, the more an individual practices it, the simpler it becomes for him to live a creative "Now" experience. He learns that everything he does is giving form to all he is. Saturn is the teacher, and holds within the greatest secrets

of the universe if one has the willingness to learn. What one
does each day is more important than what one dreams
about doing in the future. The pure essence of Saturn
speaks of reality. It separates the dream of life from what is
tangibly real, so that an individual can know his dreams,
but also realize what he must do to make them come
about. How many thousands of individuals in the world
have said thousands of times, "I could do this," or "I could
do that," with an undercurrent jealous attitude at the
fact that others have done it. Years later, these very same
individuals start living in their past, begrudging themselves
for not having done this or that correctly.

The lesson of Saturn is not to look at what others do,
or even years later what one could have done oneself, but
rather to effectively build structure to one's life, here,
now,—today!

There are many individuals who wisp through life
incapable of making decisions. The winds of chance blow
them hither and yon. At no time do they experience a solid
sense of identity, purpose, and meaningfulness to their
existence. There are other individuals who set goals for
themselves. They look at the end of something first. And
then, by considering whether or not it is worthwhile, back
up to the beginning and start working towards it.
According to Ouspensky, one of the great minds of his
day, the difference between right or wrong living is not at
all based upon the morals of society or the times one lives
in. The fact is that what is accepted as right in one society
is deemed wrong in another. And, throughout history,
what has been right in certain ages has been also deemed
wrong by others. Thus, the question of right or wrong
living, which is so important for an individual to know, is
based on something other than what society thinks or the
times one lives in. Ouspensky clearly equates it to whether
or not an individual has a goal. For the person who has no
goal, it is truly impossible to know the difference between

right or wrong. But for the person who has a goal, whatever brings him closer to his goal is right for him and whatever takes him further from it, is wrong for him. One can easily argue that if an individual's goal is wrong, then how can his actions toward it possibly be right? That is not the question here. No one but God himself can judge what is right or wrong for each individual. It is the *idea* of a goal, good or bad, right or wrong, filled with wisdom or nonsense that makes an individual know what he is doing right now is important! Thus, the idea of having goals in one's life makes it possible for a person to understand each day as an important step in the building of his evolution. It might seem that having goals tends to project individuals into the future. This is not necessarily the case. It is usually those individuals without goals who are constantly leaping into the future or, at the same time, other people's lives in order to find something tangible and meaningful for themself. The individual with goals, regardless of whether or not he will reach them, does not have to do this. He can take his life one day at a time, for he knows where he is and, whether or not the road ahead may be clear, he nevertheless knows that it is there. Thus, he functions in "The Now" according to that which is truly meaningful to him, avoiding all that which is not. In this way, he develops the art of discrimination, filtering out of his life all that would dissipate his energies, while bringing into his life the mortar from which he can build his solid foundations.

There is a cliche that says "If you want something accomplished, give the task to a person who has no time to do it, and it will be done." The truth of this lies in the fact that the individual who has no time, knows how to use time best. The delays associated with Saturn slow an individual down enough, so that instead of racing through time meaninglessly, he can learn how to fill every moment with the form and substance that will create greater meaning in his life. Though he may bog himself down in details, it is only through his willingness to accept his responsibilities of the moment that keep him contained in "The Now." The slow plodding nature of Saturn's purpose is always sure-footed and steady. This planet's energies help to effectively earth a person to his current reality.

One of the greatest detriments to living in "The Now" is man's tendency towards escapism. Each individual finds his own loopholes through which he ultimately defeats himself. Saturn is the planet of discipline. It instructs a person to stay within his own purpose, regardless of how difficult it may at times appear to be. By cooperating with Saturn's vibration, an individual learns how to establish his inner stability. He is able to build a home for himself within himself. When he can do this effectively, he will find that emotions of greed, avarice, jealousy and all other things which tend to remove oneself from oneself, have much less of an effect on him. He becomes his own sanctuary. Through this, he learns how to control his sensory impressions, and his constant reactions to the ever-changing world around him. He learns what he means to himself. Once this is accomplished he is no longer willing to compromise his "Now" for the appearance of green pastures in other people's lives that are not only beyond his reach, but which would also give him little fulfillment if he ever attained them.

Saturn is the planet of wisdom through the maturity that comes from age and experience. Some individuals are fortunate enough to understand its vibration early in life, while others do not realize the benefits of Saturn until much later. For those who are constantly asking the advice of others for each decision that they have to make, the sense of self-containment that Saturn offers never really gets established. At the same time, individuals who realize that everything meaningful in life must ultimately come from within the self, tend to make their decisions in silence without constantly seeking advice outside of themselves.

These individuals are able to develop a grip on themselves, a powerful buttress and fortress within whose walls their "Now" is forever happening. They learn the art of functioning at optimum levels, never to impress or please others, for that would be outside the wall, but rather to build a stronger sense of substance and meaning from within.

One of the easiest ways for an individual to lose his sense of "The Now" is through excessive emotion. We all go through periods in our life which are either emotionally strained or highly traumatic. Saturn is the balancer of emotion. It teaches a person how to control his emotions rather than allowing his emotions to control him. Thus, it can be a kind of emotional anchor, effectively rooting an individual in the reality of his "Now" experience. This buffers him from the harshness of unpleasant external experiences, by keeping him focused inside of himself at all times. Whatever his mission in life may be, it becomes stronger than the sensory impressions and emotions which can so easily distract him from it. This does not happen overnight, for no gain through Saturn ever does. However, it has been observed that whatever one accomplishes, constructs, or achieves through the dedication of Saturn is not easily lost.

Think what a day would be like without meaning, without purpose, without the possibility of fulfillment. This is what one's life would be like if not for Saturn. At each moment it is showing us the value of what is ours as well as our importance in a world that needs us. There are few greater meanings in life than to know that one is needed. Here is where Saturn makes an individual aware of his present duties to himself and those who need him. The ultimate that one can achieve through Saturn is the sense of meaning that comes from knowing how purposeful everything one does actually is. Once an individual knows this, he begins to see the world in a different way. The here and now consists of all that coincides with his sense of purpose and meaning. All else becomes externally filtered from his awareness. He learns not to waste time or energy on unproductive thought patterns which in the past have created roads that led to nowhere.

Now, through Saturn, he stands literally at the crossroads of life's meaning until he realizes the importance of where he stands. When this realization is reached, the individual will have the ability to feel a firm foundation within himself which affords a powerful sense of security and self-assuredness.

Thus, when we talk about "The Now," in terms of Saturn, we are talking about establishing the central theme of one's life. This planet, which rules the conscience, is forever developing in "The Now" to give an individual the steady guidance he needs in order to know his own strength. The more he cooperates with his own conscience, the more secure he is able to be within himself. Conversely, it is interesting to note that those individuals who live adversely to their conscience are filled with phobias, hypersensitivity and anxieties of all forms. Thus, Saturn can be one's benefactor, or one's burden of woe depending completely upon the ways in which a person builds his structure. While the realization of goals may be well in the future, it is what one does towards reaching them in "The Now" that creates reality.

For many, Saturn is the taskmaster. But, he who lives in "The Now" is always the master of the task!

## URANUS AND THE NOW

Uranus is the planet of awareness. It heightens and stimulates the intellect. It goes far beyond traditional thought patterns opening up an individual to new insights, discoveries and a more fascinating look on life. Of all the planets in the zodiac, the spontaneity of Uranus enables an individual to loosen his hold on the past and see the value of all that is happening in "The Now." He can change patterns of years in a single moment through the heightened awareness that Uranus gives him. This planet is considered to be the ruler of Astrology because it holds the keys of higher enlightenment within it.

Through the Uranian energy, one realizes that the world consists of many different modes of behavior, styles of life, and roads to God. One understands that the world has a place for all of them. The differences between societies, religions, and lifestyles all add color and interest to the environment. Still, the environment is the external part of one's "Now" experience. It is not the hub of the wheel from which our own ideas and thoughts emanate.

In order to be most in tune with the energy of Uranus, an individual must understand and be willing to stand for his own uniqueness. He may be of mind or character that is highly unacceptable to the society around him or the times he lives in. Nevertheless, it is his "Now." He can and, in fact, *must* be different from those around him in order to be himself. For those individuals who have clairvoyance, Uranus is the planet which enables them to tune their input to the frequency which is most comfortable for them. This enables them to filter out all undesirable and misleading premonitions, impulses, and thought streams which only confuse their personal life. Uranus as the planet of will, also enables an individual to tune his mental perceptions to another or to detune them as he wishes. In a very funny way, this is the planet that ultimately leads to a great sense of gratitude. One becomes so aware of all that life has to offer that he grows extremely thankful for whatever experiences he has. As the higher key to Mercury, Uranus helps an individual to know what he knows. Through Mercury, he thinks his thoughts, but through Uranus, he is able to observe them and understand them from a broader and more unbiased point of view. The more he can do this, the more he is able to tolerate and understand the inconsistencies he experiences.

Uranus symbolizes instaneous knowing. Its sense of vividness is the strongest of all the planets. Thus, its magnetism to the "Now" experience is extremely powerful. At the same time, the constant reversals and unexpected turns of events that one experiences are the Uranian reactions to the Karmic results of past actions. But, if an individual is impersonal in nature and does not hold onto things, he can witness every moment as a new creation.

Uranus elevates the intellect and helps to make an individual aware that within himself is the model of the entire universe. By breaking his inner barriers which limit his consciousness, he is able to see all that he is. Through such revelation, he can be aware of his own presence, rather than reaching for a sense of presence in the lives of others. This is why Uranus helps to make an individual less dependent upon others and more reliant on his own uniqueness. All of the inconsistencies that one feels within oneself are only smaller symbols of all of the apparent inconsistencies in the outside world. The more an individual can accept the diversions within himself, the easier it is for him to accept the environment he lives in. Thus, through an impersonal acceptance of all of the things that seem disharmonious with each other, man can achieve harmony with himself. If he constantly rejects all that seems disharmonious, he becomes too entrenched in his personal opinions to truly experience all that is happening in "The Now." He blocks out what he doesn't want to see, and limits the scope of his vision to only those perceptions of himself and the outside world which fit the framework of his preconceived attitudes. These atti-tudes—powerfully formed in the past—are exactly what keeps an individual in old Karmic habit-patterns that he may have long since outgrown. When he opens his consciousness to a wider perception of himself, his life begins to be filled with constant amazement. Every day he is in awe of a sense of newness that gives him what he needs to stay rooted in the present.

Perhaps one of the most beautiful aspects of Uranus is the ways in which man can use it to detach himself from emotional situations and reactions which do not allow him to see himself clearly. Uranus is a planet of clarity. It tells us that there are some things in the world that we can change, and there are others which, realistically, we have no power over. Thus, we are talking about the acceptance of change. The unexpected turns of events every day are exactly those things which lend a peculiar fascination to "The Now." They jolt an individual free from the shackles of past bondage. They illuminate his thought patterns, allowing different viewpoints, new perceptions, and changing attitudes to shake loose whatever Karma an individual has crystallized in his past.

There are many different realities, all abiding in the same universe at the same time. It is the extent to which an individual is aware of his Uranus and how to use it correctly that allows him or prevents him from experiencing the different realms of reality that exist.

Many individuals on one level or another experience a good amount of religious or spiritual Karma depending upon how they were raised in the current life, to say nothing of all they may have experienced before that. The Uranian view of religion centers around the knowing of that which is, and discards that which may be traditional, but at the same time, unrealistic. Agile ability to switch from one subject to another, one attitude to another, and one perception to another is through Uranus. The planet enables a person to be keenly aware of all that is going on in his life without becoming deeply rooted in anything. Thus, he is able to experience a wholeness within himself which, although it may seem erratic to others, allows him to flow with the current of change. The more he can do this, the better he is able to be in contact with a higher meaning to his life, rather than purposefully trying to point it in personal directions which may well be against the cosmic forces. Too many individuals believe that the term "God" is a concept handed down through the ages in books, legends, societies, and civilizations. When an individual is truly aware of Uranus, he comes in contact with the fact that there is actually a "living God," flowing through him right now in various ways, with different impulses, ideas, and understandings which give him a keen interest in himself and his universe.

In effect, Uranus is the great awakener! It shakes an individual out of the doldrums of his mundane existence and shows him a higher reality. When he starts to vibrate to this higher reality, his Karmic patterns begin to change. Much Karma can be erased when an individual is able to realize through the energies of Uranus, the importance of his impersonal self. Nearly all Karma is on a personal level. The effects of hate, greed, anger, revenge, and other negative emotions and activities that hurt mankind today exist only on the personal level. Thus, when an individual is able to see himself and his life situation in a more impersonal manner, many of these negative traits that Karmically plague him almost miraculously disappear. Instead, man becomes aware that he is part of a greater humanity, and that his function goes beyond his personal needs. His obligations are not only to himself but to the race and civilization of which his soul has chosen to be a part. The world of desire, which creates much negative Karma, becomes subservient to Uranus' clear understanding of the way things really are.

The erratic nature of this planet which leads an individual to constantly change direction is very much an important part of "The Now" experience. It enables one to feel the four winds, the three hundred and sixty degrees of the circle, the completeness of spontaneity that exists in the "Now" moment. There is no question that the Karmic lesson of Uranus is detachment! One must be involved, but not self-involved. When the personal will is surrendered to a more knowing, impersonal will then an individual begins to experience enlightenment. He can see the implications of his life, but they do not have the hold on him that they would if he was personally trying to solve his problems through the will of his lower self. When a person is able to do this, he begins to receive detached glimpses of how the universe is working. And, in some cases, he even receives instructions from higher planes as to what are the best ways in which he can make use of all that is revealed to him.

Uranus is the planet of Astrology, and to paraphrase Dane Rudhyar, Astrology's coefficient of inaccuracy is equivalent to man's coefficient of free will. Thus, man can use his free will to assert his personal desires or he can impersonally accept that which he has to experience "Now." This acceptance is very important in terms of the evolution of the human race for the more mankind can rid itself of personal greed, the more this planet will manifest its energies of impersonal love on earth. The question for each individual to ask himself is, "What am I doing right now to elevate my consciousness?" When an individual stays in constant contact with how to use his Uranian energy, then his life, his consciousness, his awareness of his impersonal self, and his importance to the world, is bound to be revealed to him. When he learns how to expect the unexpected it becomes easier for him to live in his "Now" experience. This occurs because, rather than programming himself to what his concept of enlightenment may be, he is able to leave himself open and let it be shown to him in ways which often turn out to be beyond his greatest expectations.

Uranus is the cloudbreaker. It smashes away the

vague mistiness that keeps a person from knowing himself.
It is unquestionably the destroyer of illusions. The
moment an indiviudal can see through his own illusions, he
takes a very real step towards reaching the center of
himself in "The Now."

The best way to break illusions and old karmic
habit patterns is to flow with all that is changing in the
present life current. Most individuals are so reluctant to
change that even when positive change is presented to
them, they keep trying to back up into their old ways again
and again. They do this, not because of self-denial so
much as the fact that they are used to a certain amount of
comfort in old ways. And, amazingly enough, this is so
even if the old ways meant suffering and the new ways
mean liberation.

Uranus can free a person from the past, by bringing
him new vitality, enjoyment, and an abundance of versatile
experiences in the present.

This breaks dependency relationships, as well as
thought of dependency that an individual holds in his mind.
Thus, as the forerunner of the Aquarian Age, the energies
of this planet are to be kept prominently in mind if we are to
be a race of enlightened individuals, with freedom of
thought as one of our highest moral values.

## NEPTUNE AND THE NOW:

Neptune is the planet of dreams, and dreams are
what we, on this planet, are made of. When man is born
into life, he goes into what is called "The Mystical Sleep."
All during this sleep, he dreams. From day to day and
moment to moment he lives in one dream after another;
fully believing that each is real at the time he believes it.
His life is then one big illusion. Such is also the case with
much of what he perceives around him.

Every individual likes to believe that he is
important. He goes through much effort to prove this to

his ego. Still, no matter what he accomplishes or achieves, there is an unfulfilled quantity within him because of the dream state in which he lives. Neptune's greatest power is to slowly dissolve the ego, so that man can finally see through his illusions and blend with the cosmic whole of which he is part. So long as man stays in his ego, and lives in a separated state from all that he is truly part of, he must live in a karmic condition. As an individual allows the energy of Neptune to slowly dissolve his ego, he is able to blend into a more universal oneness with himself, and the world around him. He begins to realize that he is not ruled by his body, and that the form side of life holds tremendous illusions which can constantly distract an individual from the Divine purpose. He learns the value of not thinking, rather than believing that he must think of everything all the time. Instead, he learns how to flow in the current of his life, rather than constantly trying to fight the direction of the stream he is swimming in.

Through Neptune, man is able to develop non-attachment to things. The more he can do this, the better he is able to dissolve past Karmic residue that still lingers in his life. However, this is where man's highly developed intellect often outsmarts him. He must come to understand that thoughts are things too. Before he can experience a freer, lighter sense of being, he must learn how to detach himself from his thoughts. Here, his ego goes through a great struggle. He must admit to himself that all of his thoughts are truly meaningless. This is extremely difficult because man likes to stand for principles, ideas, attitudes, and opinions which give him a sense of self-importance. At the same time, these principles, ideas, attitudes and opinions not only make past Karma cling tighter but also create more Karma for the present and the future. The "Now" is an ever-changing flow. An individual can be part of that flow only as much as he allows himself to be. He must try not to own his thoughts, but rather to allow thought to flow through him in the different ways that it changes from moment to moment and day to day. If he does this, then at any moment he is fully in touch with "The Now." And, as soon as one comes in good contact with the presence of Neptunian energy, there is a highly creative flow that begins to permeate the individual's existence. He starts to see the meaning of non-structure. He begins to understand the value of no value. He sees that all is nothing and that nothing at all is everything. Truly, his entire perspective on life changes as his perceptions are no longer distracted by the form of things. Instead, he is able to seek pure essence. As a result he starts to become in tune with his impersonal nature. When this occurs, much Karma is released, for much of the suffering that individuals go through as a result of past actions comes from their perception of themselves. When this is replaced by a more impersonal outlook on life, the dissolving effects of Neptune leave nothing for negative Karma to stay attached to. Instead the individual begins to function from his point of essence rather than his point of ego.

There is a great change in the lifestyle when one makes this realization. Outwardly, there appears to be a period of "Non-caring" which is often confused by others with either escapism or a lack of personal attention to one's loved ones and the things that seem important in everyday life. Inwardly, however, this is not what is happening. The individual is becoming in touch with the Divine nature of things, and his realization is that "Now" is forever. Here is anywhere. The concept of love, rather than being personal, starts to take on a more cosmic meaning.

The "Now" of Neptune is as formless as creation itself. It is belief in the unseeable, untouchable, intangible flowing force that is the Divine inspiration of everything that ultimately takes form. As the higher octave of Venus, Neptune is a very special form of music. It is the planet of harmony through which an individual is able to hear his own inner song that makes him part of the universe he lives in. His "Now" does not consist of the strivings of an isolated, unique ego but rather of a smooth blending of his changing identities and his eternal oneness with all that is around him.

Neptune is the planet of forgetfulness. Often this is looked upon as an extremely negative quality of the planet's energy. But if one is to stay in "The Now" the ability to forget the past becomes an extremely desirable quality. Rather than fighting shadows, illusions, and ghosts in one's mind, Neptune can be used to dissolve all that keeps a person from immersing himself totally in "The Now." Most people have a tremendous fear of losing themselves. They hold on to preconceived notions and ideas years after the utility of such notions and ideas no longer exist. They build models in their mind of how the world should be and how people in their lives should treat them. As a result, they are constantly trying to fit the world and everybody in it into the model they built at an earlier time for reasons which they probably cannot now recall. It is much easier to flow with the way things are, rather than to try to make the world fit into our conception of it.

When an individual begins to come into contact with Neptunian energies he is able to realize how much of his life is built on his imagination. People present either threats or promises to the goodness of his existence only as he imagines them. His relative state of wealth and happiness is also the total product of his imagination. His desires for esteem, recognition, importance and even his sexual drive are all the result of this same imagination. His moods and attitudes from moment to moment are all based on how he sees things. On a cloudy day, an individual will feel depressed because he is being deprived of the bright sunshine that he looks forward to. At the same time, another individual will see the clouds, but know that the sun is still shining just behind them and, therefore, will not experience the same moods as the first individual. All through life, it is man's impression of things that governs his actions and reactions. Thus, his Karma cannot go unaffected by his outlook. He takes things seriously or lightly and this depends not so much upon his individual horoscope as it does upon the actual realizations he has of himself, the universe he lives in, and the relationship between both.

There are twenty-four hours in a day, but "The Now" of Neptune says that there are no days—just one eternal flow of time through which man creates all that he imagines is possible. The "Now" of Neptune is an unspoken now. Physical words get in the way of its reality and break the continuity of its flow. For this reason, an understanding of Neptune can bring an individual a great deal of peace and harmony with himself and others. The belligerent nature of mankind, which has for thousands of years created so much hell on this earth, gets washed away by the intangible music that is Neptune's song.

Earlier, when discussing Saturn, I made mention of the fact that it is extremely important for an individual to have goals in order to stay in "The Now." The vibration of Neptune appears to contradict this but that is not so. The proper blending of the two means to have goals, and work towards them, but not be attached to their future outcome, or the past efforts one has made on their behalf. Saturn gives form to the inspiration of Neptune, and Neptune continually feeds Saturn to build more structure. From the unseen comes the seen. From the world of vision come all of the great inspirations that rise in structure in the world of form. Thus, Neptune and Saturn work together rather than contradict each other. Without Neptune's visionary qualities, the everyday, mundane, work-world reality of Saturn would have little meaning;

with it there is reason, purpose and inspiration which makes "The Now" exciting!

## PLUTO AND THE NOW:

As the planet of endings, Pluto plays a very important role in the "Now" experience. By using Pluto correctly, an individual is able to end lingering thoughts from the past by divorcing himself from any importance he once attached to them.

At the same time, Pluto has much to do with man's unconscious nature. It surfaces all the hidden thoughts and feelings which must be eliminated in order to make room for the new. When an individual does not use his Pluto, he tends to hold onto many old thought and habit patterns which keep his life going in the same self-destructive circles that he instinctively hates.

In the same way that an individual throws his garbage out every day, there are thoughts that have to be discarded also. If they are not, then they swim forever in a person's unconscious, from time to time rising to the conscious level and influencing behavior patterns much against the conscious will.

Pluto is the planet of decisions. We tend to suffer for many years until we are able to make finalized decisions about things. We collect more and more information to help us make these decisions, but the failure to make them only burdens us more and more with all of the information we have collected. Once we can make final decisions on things, all of the collected information that we gathered to help us make such decisions miraculously drops off. Instead, we are free to go into new experiences with fresh attitudes.

The "Now" exists on many levels. Pluto is a planet of great depth and wisdom. Without using it, an individual only sees the surface of things. He misses the undercurrent stream that is at the roots of all creativity. A great deal of this undercurrent exists on sexual levels, which man must learn how to get in touch with in order to understand where the roots of his tree stem from.*

Fulfillment of the unconscious sexual drive is one of the strongest motivating factors in "The Now." It seeks expression nearly all the time, but for reasons of society, religion, social acceptibility and childhood training, most people tend to go around it, rather than confronting their very real sexual needs. They go through life frustrated and never really quite know why. As the ruler of mass consciousness, it becomes very obvious that no matter how much people are uniquely different from each other, the one thing that they share in common is their "lower nature." In order for an individual to be happy in the "Now" he must confront his lower nature, accept it, realize that he is not "perfect," and then learn how to live with himself and his "base" desires (which, incidentally, he sees in others more readily than he sees in himself).

The "Now" is constantly transforming itself every day. All over the world there are great social sweeping changes. People are moving from one place to another, changing their jobs, getting married and getting divorces. An acceptance of the fact that the world consists of great social change makes it easy for an individual to be part of "The Now" experience. If a person keeps trying to relate to himself and others in the same ways he always has, he truly misses the sense of presence that the "Now" affords. There is an expression that "rules are made to be broken." This is quite true; for if they were not broken, there would be absolutely no way of creating new and better ones. This

---

* See *The Astrology of Sexuality* by Martin Schulman, publ. Samuel Weiser, Inc., 1978, N.Y.

accounts for the very natural desire in man to be destructive, to different degrees, of the rules society puts on him. He constantly questions their validity, measuring it against ideas he has that he thinks might be better. Thus, there is good reason for each individual to get in touch with his destructive instincts. From these destructive instincts, come the building blocks of future creation. If a person denies his destructive nature, then he does not get fully in touch with his complete vision of things in the world around him.

There is a dynamic quality to Pluto that represents the strength an individual has in his convictions. When a person believes in truth, he is literally willing to go through "hell" to defend and fight for his beliefs. This is the proper use of Pluto. It strengthens attitudes, beliefs and ideas making an individual willing to tear apart all that contradicts what he knows.

Too many of us have a tendency to go back over things long after we have made decisions about them. Pluto closes chapters in one's life never again to be re-opened. The day an individual graduates from school he has a Pluto-like feeling. He cannot go back, for he has already done that. Instead, he must move on to something new. Often that something new has not fully taken form in his mind yet. Thus, Pluto has that kind of unknown quality to it that tends to make people a little fearful of starting new patterns. Still, they must! And, the interesting thing is that they invariably do, as soon as they realize that the past has little bearing on reaching fulfillment in "The Now."

Pluto is also a planet of great wealth. Deep within oneself lie all the hidden talents, abilities, and plans for the future that make "The Now" a constantly regenerative experience, if one would only reach for them. The lonely quality of Pluto exists only so that a person can get in touch with his true inner self rather than trying to find himself in the mirrors of everybody he comes into contact with.

With firmness and strength, Pluto tears asunder what is no longer useful, making the "Now" happen. At different stages in our lives we find ourselves thrust out of one nest after another, so that we can learn new things rather than hide in the old. These are Plutonian experiences, and we should be grateful for them because they help us to evolve.

When an individual loses a job, he feels that he is cut off from his line of support (financially). When a marriage breaks, a person feels that he is cut off from his emotional security and his dreams. When a person moves, he feels that he is cut off from all that was familiar to him. When a friendship ends, an individual feels that he is cut off from another individual who accepted him and his ideas. In all of these instances and many more, the constantly eroding force of Pluto dries up each riverbed in order to force an individual to seek the next clear pool of water to bathe in.

As a result, Pluto is the prime mover of the human race. It creates through destruction, much like the tearing down of an old building so that a new one can be built in the same place. It symbolizes progress, and a deep feeling of movement in "The Now."

From the very bowels of the earth, it brings forth all of the upheavals that regenerate mankind into a better race. The Bible says "Thou Shalt Not Kill," but that is an incorrect translation. What it really says is "Thou Shalt Not Murder." There is a big difference between the two. Murder is the willful intent to destroy another for personal reasons. Killing may sometimes be necessary in order to preserve life. We see this in wars, but even in much smaller ways, we often cut back the branches of a plant so that the rest of the plant can survive. If we find roaches in our home, we kill them (perhaps with a little bit of inner sorrow that we have to) so that they do not poison our food. Thus, Pluto has to be put in its proper perspective. We must kill old thoughts that are destructive to our enjoyment of "The Now." And, sad as this may sometimes be, it is the only way that we can survive in our very real "Now" experience.

Pluto symbolizes the completion of Karma. Every time we finish one phase of our life, we no longer have Karma with that aspect of our being. Our inner consciousness changes. Then we are ready to begin Karma with another phase that we have not yet tasted.

As a result, far from being the ominous malefic that it has been pictured as, Pluto symbolizes fruition. It may be the completion of a dream, the attainment of success, the reaching of a goal etc. The problem that most people have with it is that once one reaches these things, one has to find new perceptions of success, new goals to set, and new dreams to dream. And, interestingly enough, one always does! And, the reason for this is because "The Now" is forever happening. It may not always have the appearance we thought it would have, because that changes. Still, there is always something new to replace something old.

In order to accept his, an individual has to be willing to see himself as a new being. Experiences automatically create changes in our structure. Most people try to hold on to their old identities even while they are attaining new ones which better fit the environment in their current "Now" experience. Once one realizes that identity is a product of what one does, and who one relates to, then the Plutonian changes that effect one's life can be taken in stride and appreciated for all the amazing wonders that they bring!

# ALLEGORY

Once there was a man who had reached the middle of his life. He decided that it was time to contemplate his worth and evaluate his direction. So, leaving his friends, his family, and most of his earthly possessions behind him, he trod off into the woods where he could think undisturbed.

When he entered the woods, he didn't know if he was doing the right thing, but he knew he had to do it. At first the beauty of his new surroundings filled him with awe and wonder. Soon he leaned how to listen to the sounds of nature and as weeks turned into months he slowly found himself changing. Every now and again he missed the people he had left behind, but the great beauty of his new environment lured him further into the mystery he was seeking. and he could not turn back.

In time, he learned how to listen to his own thoughts. He could see his mind in the trees and feel his emotions in the bushes. The perfect balance of nature that surrounded him was starting to become him. The fighting that used to go on within himself was slowly beginning to disappear. At first he was frightened for although he hadn't realized it, the turmoils to which his mind was accustomed had kept him company. Now they were gone, and instead there was only the great stillness of nature.

More time passed and he began to realize that he could no longer categorize the people about whom he used to hold opinions. He began to see the unimportance of classifying all the little things that used to trouble him. Now he had a different problem. With a clear mind, empty of wearisome worries that had always vexed his spirit, what was he to do? In the past, the voices of others with their strong opinions had somehow guided him. The effects of other people's lives had impinged upon his own so much that he never really had to concern himself with the direction his life should take.

After two years in the woods, he began to wonder if the outside world had changed much. He thought of the people he had known, wondered what they would be like now. Then, he discovered an amazing thing about the change that had taken place within himself. All he had to do was to think of a person and somehow, through some strange miracle, he instantly knew what the person was like now. At first, he found this difficult to believe but after a while he discovered what the woods had done to him. He could touch a leaf and know when it was going to rain. He could somehow sense the presence of even the smallest of animals hundreds of yards away. And, always, he would be right. Something had brought him in tune with the perfect harmony of nature. The slightest upset in the ecological balance to which he had grown accustomed would instantly attract his attention.

For the first time in his life he realized that he was a part of God's creation. He had read about this state of being in books. He had secretly dreamed of it, but this was different. He was actually participating in reality.

He sat down and leaned against the trunk of a giant Sequoia tree to contemplate. Somehow, in ways which he did not understand, he had put himself through years of emotional torture. Then he had tested his ability and his desire to survive amidst the natural elements which were unfamiliar to him. And, much to his amazement, here he was, intact after all. Would he spend the rest of his life in the forest, or would he in time go out to meet people like he had in the past? The question perplexed him, because he knew he could never tell anybody about what he had found. In some ways he was frightened that the strength of the people's desires would bring him back to all he had discarded. Still, after two years in the woods he was growing lonesome. It was not the same kind of loneliness he had known before his journey. He longed for the sounds of nature in people. The long months alone had made him silent. He wanted to share what he had found with others, but he also knew that he must preserve it for himself.

He remembered how it had once seemed so important to try to reform the world, or perhaps redeem it from some vague, impending doom. Now, he did not have the same feeling. He had found his identity amidst the trees and the flowers. He had witnessed how everything in nature fulfills itself in its season. He, too, was now filled with the abundant joys of nature. For months he compared everything he felt in the woods with what he knew he would feel from people.

Here in the woods, he watched each moment renew itself through the vividness of the ever-happening Now. Regardless of the weather or the changing days, there was great peace inside. He picked up a tiny flower and stared at it. Somehow, he knew the flower would be able to answer him. Without words the flower filled him with joy. And he realized that it was doing this without losing any beauty of its own. But, he had picked the flower and he knew it could grow no more. This saddened him. If only he had been able to get his answer by looking at the flower without picking it from its natural habitat. . . Then he became enlightened.

If he left the forest to enlighten others, he would be removing himself from his natural source. How long could he endure? Like the flower he could only bloom for a while and then fade. He decided it would be wiser to stay within his source. The Now, after all, was not something to boast of, or even to lead others to, but rather to experience for oneself. He smiled as he thought, "Let all who want to know venture into the forest themselves, where deep within the recesses of their minds and hearts they will feel the wind, taste the rain, and let the gentle wisdom of natural law guide their journey."

# CONCLUSION

The laws of Karma are extremely simple and very profound at the same time. Thoughts, words and actions both create and resolve Karma.

Perhaps the single greatest cause of most Karmic conditions stems from the opinions and attitudes that an individual possesses. Thus, one of the easiest ways to resolve Karma is to learn how to loosen one's hold on fixed opinions and attitudes which may or may not be true. We always find that life is a process of learning and unlearning. Every time we learn something new, we are either reinforcing or letting go of something old. When we have major realizations we often discover that attitudes and opinions which we have held for many years are no longer true for us.

In Volume I of this series (The Moon's Nodes and Reincarnation), Karma is seen in terms of duality of experience. In one's basic essence the truth is known but, through interaction with one's environment and the bargains one has made with others in order to survive, somehow the truth is often lost. Expediency takes the place of meaning and purpose. Thus, a re-evaluation of all one is and is not is the first step towards understanding the direction of one's Karma. In the first book, the individual is shown how to close or how far he is from his ideals, and wha he must do with his life in order to reach them.

Volume II (Retrogrades and Reincarnation) holds a mystical secret that was purposely not mentioned. The most important manifestation of Retrograde Planets occurs through unconscious levels. As a person becomes more in touch with the Retrograde vibration, he begins to experience what his inner self is about. The outer world with all of its magnetic temptations (which often remove one from onself) becomes less important. In this sense, the purpose of Astrology, which is to help an individual grow through understanding, can be fulfilled.

One of the problems most individuals experience in attempting to change their lives is that they try to consciously change what is unconscious. Naturally, this is impossible. The unconscious can be changed only through its own medium. The conscious mind can go through thousands of affirmations, prayers, resolutions and subtle attempts to change one's being, but it is only when the conscious mind makes contact with the unconscious mind that change is really possible.

Volume I shows the conscious mind what changes are desirable. Volume II opens unconscious channels to receive the information from Volume I. At this point, it is important to realize that for most people, the process of getting in touch with the unconscious mind is rather frightening. In whatever way the conscious mind sees the self and its place in the world, the unconscious mind will tend to exaggerate that view. What appears good to the conscious seems to be pure nirvana to the unconscious. What seems distasteful to the conscious often appears as a veritable nightmare to the unconscious. This is because the conscious mind is govered by the superego which puts limits and boundaries on what it is willing to experience. The unconscious requires years of training before it will accept such limitations. As a rule, the unconscious mind is an ambling stream that knows few, if any, boundaries.

It is for this reason that most people when they first are able to see their unconscious mind feel as if they are going "insane." They see and experience things that they know nobody would ever accept. One must deal with broken word streams, alphabetical associations, categorical arrangements, distorted pictures, sounds, colors, voices, and for the most part, what appears to be a conglomeraton of fragmented nonsense. If one learns to watch these things rather than react to or identify with them, answers to long-asked questions slowly begin to emerge. Perhaps the most important thing to remember in dealing with the unconscious mind is that the methods used by the conscious mind do not work.

The conscious mind likes to speculate and guess. The unconscious mind does not accept such false methods of thinking. Thus, one must teach the conscious mind not to speculate or guess or draw premature conclusions from what the unconscious mind is showing it. The unconscious mind often shows itself when it is sure of conscious acceptance.

When the conscious mind accepts the unconscious, then great transformations begin. A reprogramming process can be consciously initiated. As long as the unconscious feels safe, it will cooperate. It is important to realize that the process of transformation of the unconscious is a tediously slow one. It often takes many years, and one should not expect great results over-night. The rewards, however, greatly outweigh the effort.

As the process of transformation is going on, it is natural for one to feel deprived of all that everyone else is experiencing in the outer world. Volume III of the series (Joy and the Part of Fortune) shows what a person can look forward to when they are ready to come out of themselves. It represents a balance between the deep inner work that is going on and the state of happiness that awaits them when it is completed. It enables an individual to stay in contact *here,* while at the same time returning the unconscious.

During the process of transformation, it is important to understand the Part of Impersonal Consciousness (mentioned in Volume III). The Part of Impersonal Consciousness helps one to differentiate on unconscious levels all of those things in the world which are personal from those which are not. The more an individual is able to make these differentiations, the greater his evolutionary progress will be. One cannot serve two masters. Many people become too involved with things that do not personally concern them and, as a result, have little energy or ability to focus their attention on all that does.

As an individual begins to integrate the inner realms with the outer world, he begins to see more and more the importance of discrimination. And, the better he can discriminate, the more happiness he will experience in his personal life. After months or years of practice, one slowly begins to reach enlightenment. At first, it comes in isolated moments, but eventually the moments become longer until ultimately after many years of effort the moments connect with each other.

When this occurs, a new level of consciousness is reached. The problems of elemental karma begin to fade into the past which in reality no longer exists. At first, one tends to experience a great sense of loneliness, for the mind companions to the self were always karmic problems. At this new level, the mind begins to clear the waste it was carrying for years and, perhaps, lifetimes. The biggest difficulty an individual faces at this point is truly finding what to do with himself. He can no longer be motivated by guilt, fear, feelings of inadequacy, money, the attitudes and opinions of others, and the unconscious voices in his memories. Many at this point (called "The Now") seem to be quite perplexed. They feel a great inner peace as the racing of their minds starts to quiet. However, as is always the case with growing, there is a strong desire to go backwards, hiding in the shadow of what was uncomfortable enough to prompt them to seek new levels, but still seems vaguely familiar.

While this book is an attempt to explain how to live in the Now, the reader must understand that only through experiencing it can one achieve the knowledge of it. There is no suffering in the Now because it is a state of harmony with nature. Rather than constantly fighting the natural forces that exist, one learns how to flow with them and, in essence, becomes one with them: first by accepting the outer world and everything in it, and then by understanding how all personal reality is controlled through the inner self. There is Karma in the Now, but it is not like time karma which constantly repeats itself in old patterns and habits. The Karma of the Now involves the efforts of the individual to stay centered and balanced amidst whatever is. It is important to realize that although we tend to think that we cannot achieve this, we truly can simply through our faith, our knowing and our understanding that Now is all there is.

---

This is the last book in the *Karmic Astrology* series. As the information in these books was given as a gift to me, so let it now be yours, so that the journey that starts with seeing yourself can proceed to meeting yourself and each day move one step closer to being yourself. Once this is achieved, much less focus of attention is needed on the self, and you will truly begin to fulfill your cosmic destiny by being in the Now.